The CX EDGE

Customer Experience Questions to Help You
ATTRACT, KEEP and WOW Customers

Jeff Tobe, M.Ed, CSP

Customer Experience Systems
5311 Friendship Avenue,
Pittsburgh PA 15224
www.JeffTobe.com

Contact us about bulk pricing on orders of 25 or more books.

Print ISBN: 978-0-578-97068-4

Printed in the United States of America

First Edition

TABLE OF CONTENTS

Jeff Tobe, M.Ed, CSP

PROLOGUE

WHY IS STARBUCKS so successful at selling you a $4.00 cup of coffee when McDonald's charges $2.00?

Why does a stay at a Ritz-Carlton hotel seem much different than a stay at the Holiday Inn?

Most people today would answer that it's all about "customer service" when, in fact, they would be wrong! Both McDonald's and Holiday Inn offer incredible customer service. What Starbucks and Ritz-Carlton understand is that it is about the customer EXPERIENCE!

Throughout this book, I will use the word "customer" to make sure that, no matter what you do for a living, you understand that we all have internal and external customers. I would hope that everyone in your organization can define external customer. I define '**internal customer**', however, as '*anybody without whom we can't do what we do every single day*'. This may be a paradigm shift for many of you. For example, my FedEx driver is an internal customer. If he doesn't show up on the days that I need him to pick up my parcels, I am out of business. So, he is a vital part of what I do every day.

So here is the problem on which this book is focused. Customer "*experience*" has become the new buzz word in the corporate world and I am not sure that most professional organizations really understand it. "*Service*" is what you offer your customers—internal and external—everyday as a trained professional; it is personal and it comes from the heart. The nurse who truly cares about her patients. The sixth-grade teacher who customizes her lesson plan for each student. The postal delivery person who takes time out of a busy schedule to help an elderly woman take down her Christmas decorations.

I am often asked if customer service is dead. It's not dead, but it is just not the differentiator it used to be. While your competitors are competing on service, why wouldn't you look to the next plateau—EXPERIENCE? Customer *experience* is about considering our customers' experiences from the minute they make contact with our organization until the minute they are done. This involves so many more people than just you.

Those organizations who purposefully examine every customer *touch point*—those opportunities we have to influence the customer, from the parking attendant to our on-hold message, to accounting, to our website and many more—are those who will excel at the customer experience. By driving the message of the experience through every department, people realize that, no matter their title or contribution—part time or full time—they are part of the customer experience, and they start to become more engaged. By having everyone on your team, or in the organization itself, consider their specific customer touch points and how they can better that one experience, they automatically become more engaged at what they do and, ultimately, the customer is the one who benefits. Imagine a CPA meeting with a client (touch point) and hearing about a problem that's outside of their realm of expertise. They don't hesitate to suggest that someone else in the firm could help with that challenge. That CPA has just engaged that client at a whole different level because of taking advantage of one simple touch point.

The experience has to start with you! Because of your influence and because you touch so many different people at so many levels of the organization, you have to step up to the plate as the leader you are. It starts with you talking to as many people as you can, walking around asking critical questions like, *"What is the (fill in the name of your organization here) experience?"* Then, figure out how to shatter the stereotype of the experience customers EXPECT to have with you, your department, or with your organization. Ask yourself, *"What small touch point could I focus on this week that will ultimately shatter that stereotype?"*

Imagine going to a new restaurant that has been touted as the best in town. You arrive at 7:50 p.m. for an 8:00 p.m. reservation and are seated right on time. You go on to have the best service and possibly the best food you have ever eaten. At one point, the chef comes out to your table and explains how each of your dishes was prepared. The manager checks on you a few times. It is perfect. After dinner, you proceed to go outside, you proffer your parking ticket to the car valet, and FIFTY-FIVE MINUTES later your car arrives! Isn't that part of the overall experience? Of course it is. But, let's take this to the next step. It is now three months later and you have told hundreds of people to go to that new restaurant because the food is amazing and the service is outstanding. Then, you finish with one word. **BUT!** "...*BUT your car will take forever to get to you after dinner.*"

What's this got to do with YOUR profession? Everything! The minute we get our people asking critical questions like "*What comes after the BUT?*" is the minute we start to become 100% customer centric. "*They are the nicest people to work with BUT they always are late on delivery.*" "*You should call my lawyer because she is great BUT she charges too much.*" "*They are amazing caregivers to my Mom BUT the place smells terrible.*" We need to examine every touch point and imagine what the customer might say. To start making the critical shift from service to experience, begin by examining those touch points and seeing the world through THEIR eyes, not yours.

Each chapter in this book does NOT have a title but rather, it poses a critical question. In an ideal world, you would gather your team and answer each of the questions posed. In a not-so-ideal-but-acceptable world, you will ponder the question before I answer it in each chapter.

I am getting ahead of myself. Let's go back and start at the beginning...

CRITICAL QUESTION #1

Why should you start thinking about shifting
from customer SERVICE to customer
EXPERIENCE?

LET'S TALK ABOUT customer service! It just has not been discussed, dissected, and examined enough over the last few years (hint of sarcasm there!). In visiting my local bookstore (and YES, we still have one), I realized that there are more books written on customer service than any other business topic today. The sad part is that I also realized I have read many of them.

Don't get me wrong. There's probably not a more important topic than the 'service' we offer our clients, patients, or members, but I think things have changed. Those organizations that recognize the next wave in customer service will be the ones who ultimately 'serve' their market better than any others. When you think of organizations the likes of Nordstrom, Zappos, and USAA, we automatically think that customer service is the one thing that separates them from the pack. This is not entirely true.

Imagine for a moment that I have a handful of coffee beans in my palm. I take those beans to my local McDonald's and they make me a coffee for about $1.25. Now, take those same beans (alright, maybe you can argue that they are a little better-quality bean, but that's inconsequential in this illustration) over to this relatively-new phenomenon called Starbucks, and they make me a cup of coffee for about $3.00. Is the service really any different at Starbucks versus McDonald's? As a matter of fact, the senior citizens at my McDonald's are the friendliest, most accommodating people I know. No, it's gone beyond customer service.

Continuing on with our handful of coffee beans...

Awhile back, I had the fortuitous opportunity to spend a few days of R&R on the island of Bali in the South Pacific. Add to that the splendor of the Four Season's Resort—a five-star hotel—rated in 2014 as one of the top five resorts in the ENTIRE world. Our private, thatched roof, dining room—open on three sides to the beach and the Pacific—was the setting for breakfast each morning. Remember our coffee beans? A cup of coffee at the Four Season's Hotel cost something in the neighborhood of $7.00. AND WE PAID IT! Why?

You see, it wasn't the service, although I have NEVER had service as personalized and attentive as we did at this resort. But breakfast, once delivered to our villa, was still just a meal! No, it was THE EXPERIENCE. People are more than willing to pay for the experience if it is unique, personalized, and responsive. When was the last time you considered the experience that your clients have with you each time they interact with your organization? What is the experience at EVERY touch point you have with your customer?

> *"We don't determine what good service is. The customer does."*
>
> *— Nordstrom newsletter*

Back in the 1980s, one of my first consulting clients was a Seattle-based department store chain by the name of Nordstrom. On our first meeting, the leadership group with which I was working decided that they were going to offer "knock-your-socks-off" customer service when their customer had a problem.

So, what happened? By the end of the 1980s, it didn't matter what profession we were in; we were all walking around saying something to the effect of, *"We are going to solve our customer's problems beyond their expectations."*

Fast forward to the 1990s when I got to work with a small car company by the name of Saturn. (It's even SMALLER today. No testament to my work!) I had Saturn leadership study the Nordstrom model. They concluded that just solving their customer's problem was not good enough. They determined that they were going to offer "knock-your-socks-off" customer service ALL OF THE TIME. Not just when their customer had a problem. They decided that they were going to be the 'customer service car company.'

The problem is that most organizations I encounter worldwide, are still stuck in offering amazing customer service.

To start to make a shift from service to experience, begin by examining those touch points and see the world through THEIR eyes not yours.

Gaylord Opryland gives guest a hotel-exclusive clock radio

Christina McMenemy had stayed at the Gaylord Opryland resort three years in a row[3] for the annual BlissDom conference.

On her first visit, she noticed lovely, relaxing music playing in her hotel room when she first walked in. It sounded like something you'd hear in a high-end spa. She realized it was coming from the clock radio that doubled as a sound machine.

Throughout the weekend, Christina noticed how relaxed she felt when the music was playing. It was the best sleep she'd had in ages!

She loved that clock radio. So before she checked out, she asked the hotel where she could buy one for herself.

Unfortunately the hotel didn't sell them, but they gave her the model number and said she could find one in any store. She took that model number from store to store for two years but could never find one that had the spa sounds. It was looking like the clock radio she wanted was a hotel-exclusive.

During her third stay at the resort, Christina had just about given up hope but decided to try her luck on Twitter. Here's how it went:

Christina from OH
@mommystory

@GaylordOpryland Where can I buy this Sharper Image clock radio in my room? None in stores have the "spa" sounds & I've never slept better!

Gaylord Opryland Resort
@GaylordOpryland

Replying to @mommystory

@mommystory Unfortunately, our version isn't available to the public, but here is a Shaper Image alarm clock like it: amzn.to/ADMXzL.

Christina from OH
@mommystory

Replying to @GaylordOpryland

@GaylordOpryland Yeah, that one doesn't have the spa sound. Been looking for one after loving the 1 in my room for 3yr now at Blissdom. :(

So that was that. Christina had officially given up.

She spent the evening at the conference closing party and came back to her room for the night. To her surprise, she found a second clock radio sitting on the dresser and an envelope with her name on it:

"Christina, Thank you for following us on Twitter. We hope you enjoy these spa sounds at home. If you need anything, please let us know. Sincerely, Elizabeth, Nick & Tori."

Needless to say, Christina was very excited and appreciated the resort's kind gesture. "You reaffirmed that there are still companies out there focused on great service, and you've made a lifelong fan out of me. And you're now helping me get some of the best sleep possible, year-round, which any mother will tell you is a feat worthy of high praise."

The Takeaway

Going "above and beyond" for your customers is a commonly discussed <u>cus-tomer service best practice</u>—and a great way to increase your <u>customer reten-</u>

tion. Why is that important? Because improving your customer retention can directly impact your bottom line in a very positive way. One study showed that just a 5% improvement in customer retention can actually bump profits up by a whopping 25%.[4]

And if you're serious about customer retention, you'll want to keep track of your customer's relationship with your business. This means having all their relevant details in one place that anyone on your customer service team can access.

For example, RingCentral's identity merge tool gives you a complete picture of your customer based on their previous interactions with your team. That way, whoever is helping out the customer at any given moment can pull up the customer's full history and provide a more personalized experience.

Gaylord Opryland recognized a valuable opportunity to turn a longtime customer into a customer for life. And they looked great in the process. The hotel also recognized the need to go beyond customer service and consider the customer experience.

We have to ask ourselves, "What is the story the customer (in this case, Christina from OH) will tell when they are done working with us?"

CRITICAL QUESTION #2

What's The Difference Between Service and
Experience?

AS I TRAVEL the world speaking, training, and consulting with organizations in hundreds of different industries and spheres of influence, I have been surprised that the question, *"What is the difference between customer SERVICE and customer EXPERIENCE?"* still stumps even the most-savvy CEO!

Customer service is what you should already be doing well. It comes from the heart. *"What can I do for you?"* *"How can I help you?"* If you customer service is outstanding, then this is just a given with your people. If it's not top notch, then you need to do something RIGHT NOW to make it right. Reading this book is a good first step and perhaps you need to go back to basics and re-examine your customer service journey.

The unfortunate thing is that customer service is no longer a differentiating factor in the marketplace. I can almost guarantee that, if I were to ask your competitors what sets them apart, they are going to tell me customer service. It's not your products or your services that set you apart and it is certainly not your customer service!

Customer service is the assistance a company provides to customers before, during, and after purchasing or using its products or services. Good customer service leaves customers satisfied and involves creating bonds with customers, with the aim of developing them into long-term relationships. According to Study.com, some elements of good customer service include:

- Professionalism: You need to treat all your customers professionally. Professionalism makes customers feel cared for.

- Promptness: You must meet customers' expectations with regards to delivery timelines. Avoid delays at all costs. This includes replying to customer messages promptly.

- Politeness: Whether the customer makes a purchase or not, it's important to remain polite. Greeting the customer appropriately and saying *"thank you very much"* are a part of good customer service.

- Personalization: Every customer feels good when the company they are doing business with addresses them on a personal level.

A good customer experience means the company has provided great customer service, and that the service offered has left the customer happy and satisfied with the service received. I don't know about you BUT, I am no longer settling for a SATISFIED customer. That brings us to the question *"What exactly is the difference between customer service and customer experience (CX)?"*

Customer experience (by my definition) is the ability to step back and ask ourselves that critical question, *"What is my customer's experience from the minute they make contact with us until the minute they are done?"* This involves so many more people than the one who is offering great service. This sounds easier than it is. We can look at the customer experience journey from the minute they sign on to our website until they sign off. A financial planner might examine the journey from the minute the young twenty-five-year-old client signs on to their services until their death 75 years later. And, my plumber might consider the journey from the minute a potential client calls until the leaky faucet is fixed.

You see, it is a personalized experience for your specific business or organization.

Simply put, customer experience is the perception the customer has of your brand. It's how customers perceive their interactions with your company or brand. While you may think your customer experience and brand is the same thing, a customer may have a different perception, and that would be regarded as the customer experience.

Customer experience is not restricted to how many interaction mediums you have, and it's also not to be confused with a once-off experience. It is the overall experience a customer has across platforms where they can engage with your company, measured across an entire purchase cycle.

A company may focus on certain parts of the customer journey but may fail to impress the customer on other aspects. That results in a customer experience that is weak due to ignoring an aspect of the customer's journey. For example, a customer may have a wonderful experience when purchasing a product but have a negative experience when requiring assistance from customer service. That happens when you don't pay attention to all aspects of the customer journey.

There is a fine line between customer service and customer experience. Customer experience actually encompasses customer service. Customer service is limited to one aspect of the customer's journey. This is when the customer is experiencing some sort of issue with your product or service. When a business assists the customer with the help they require, it's good customer service.

Customer experience, however, is more extensive. It's understanding how your customer is feeling and what they're thinking every single time they interact with your business, from the moment they're aware you exist. It involves every aspect of what a company has to offer, including how its customer care is rated, packaging, product and service features, reliability, ease of use, and other elements.

Customer service is reactive, whereas customer experience is proactive. When you are reactive to your customers, you're not preventing disasters from occurring, you are simply fixing what needs to be fixed once it has taken place. When you are proactive with your customers, it's taking the time to analyze what issues may potentially arise and stopping them from taking place before they do. In my last book, *ANTICIPATE: Knowing What Customers Need Before They Do* (John Wiley & Sons) I made it clear that with customer experience, the business' objective is to provide customers with a better overall experience, which leads to happier customers by anticipating those issues that might arise.

"Customer Experience is understanding how your customer is feeling and what they're thinking every single time they interact with your business, from the moment they're aware you exist."

What Customer Experience Is Not

- Customer experience is not a department: Every team in your organization, from marketing and sales to customer support, should be involved in the customer experience.

- Customer experience isn't reactive: As previously mentioned, you don't wait for the customer to raise an issue to resolve their problem or meet their requirements. To provide customers with a great CX, companies need to become intuitive, learn from previous or common issues, and get a better understanding of the customer's needs and expectations...ANTICIPATE!

With today's evolving customer expectations, your company may excel at providing satisfactory customer service; however, delivering great customer experience is not easy. Another way to explain the differences is with an example of a customer journey where a new client opens a checking account online or through a chatbot assistant but finishes the process in a branch or over the phone with a representative. If the representative is friendly and helpful, he or she delivers good customer service. The frictionless process of opening an account online or having a chatbot assistant to check their account balance and recent transactions helps create a great customer experience. Positive customer experiences like this have grown from a nice-to-have to a necessity in every industry. Each task completed, and the time in which it's done, can greatly impact the overall success of CX efforts.

Moving beyond customer experience, if customers find it easy to do business with you and experience **consistent**, high-quality experiences every time through every touch point, then you are moving from customer experience to **customer excellence**. Perhaps this is the subject of my next book?

Nordstrom is known for their amazing customer service, but they go beyond just serving their customers. Let me share a personal story that took place quite a few years ago, and yet, I share it with audiences around the world.

I was living in Dallas, Texas, at a time when Nordstrom only had one store in the Galleria shopping mall. I was meeting a prospective client at a restaurant in the mall but arrived early. I decided I would stop in at Nordstrom to see if they carried a certain brand of running shoe in which I was interested. The clerk approached me and, rather than saying those excruciating four words, "Can I help you?", he proffered his hand for me to shake and introduced himself as Jake.

Jake proceeded to tell me that he was a "shoe authority" and if I had any questions, he was "the man." I laughed as I told him exactly which style of shoe I was in search of. Jake confirmed that Nordstrom did indeed carry the brand. He immediately offered me a seat, asked me my foot size and told me he would return in minutes.

True to his promise, Jake reappeared only minutes later with a very disappointed look on his face. He explained that although they carried the shoe I desired, they did not have it in my size. He suggested that he could order it from another store—specifically one in Oklahoma City because, remember, Dallas only had this one flagship Nordstrom at the time.

I thanked him and told him that there was no immediacy and that I would find them elsewhere. That's when Jake asked the question, "Mr. Tobe, how long are you going to be in the mall?" I explained that I had to meet a client and would be about 90 minutes. He then asked me if I would do him a favor and return to the store immediately following my lunch. I agreed.

Upon returning to the store, Jake galloped toward me with a big smile on his face. "I've got them" he repeated several times. I asked him how he possibly could have secured the shoes, but he refused to answer and just ushered me to a chair to try on the shoes.

As Jake unpacked the shoe box, I noticed a bright red sticker with a "Foot Locker" logo on it. When I inquired about this, my over-zealous shoe authority explained that he had traveled the length of this giant mall to see if any of his competitor's carried the shoes in my size. When he came across one that did, he purchased the shoes himself and now offered them to me like a proud bird dog offering its prey.

The next thing I noticed is that the price tag from Foot Locker was $1.50 more than for what Nordstrom had them listed. Jake would have no part of my paying extra. His next statement proved that customer experience is about creating a loyal customer. He said, "When you think of purchasing shoes, I want you to think of me."

Needless to say, I purchased all of my shoes from Jake over the next few years. He could have offered me wonderful customer service, but he chose to consider my end-to-end experience and the story he wanted me to tell others when I walked away.

CRITICAL QUESTION #3

WHY Customer Experience?

I AM SURE you have heard of the Gallup Organization. Most likely, you have heard their name associated with political polls. If you look at their website, they are actually *"a global analytics and advice firm that helps leaders and organizations solve their most pressing problems."* Each year, since 2013, Gallup has done an engagement survey worldwide. In the U.S., it's called "State of the American Workforce." In 2020, they found that only 33% of American workers are engaged at what they do in the workplace compared to 70% worldwide!

It's pathetic! It means that 67% of Americans go to work to get their paycheck. Now, **don't confuse employee SATIS-FACTION with employee ENGAGEMENT**. They are happy to get their checks. They will even tell you that they love working for the organization. They are just not engaged.

I have given you the first (and major) reason to change your entire organization's mindset to that of customer experience. In working with hundreds of organizations over the years, I am confident that when companies make the leap from customer service, and settling for a satisfied customer, to customer experience, they incur both LOYAL external customers *and* ENGAGED employees. We have also proven that the more engaged people are internally, the better the experience externally.

So, why not focus internally and get your people more engaged at what they do? In Critical Question 5, we will discuss employee engagement and a simple exercise you can do right away to engage your employees.

BUT...there are some other important reasons to consider CX.

1. **Customer loyalty is more important now than ever before.**

Companies across the world have an average customer satisfaction rate of 86%.

Customer experience is key to exceeding your customers' expectations. Brands have to be accurate, dependable, and provide the service they promise. The opportunity lies in the ability to deliver what you promised and surprise, wow, and delight your customer with extra care and support.

A loyal customer contributes 2.6 times as much revenue as a somewhat satisfied customer, and 14 times as much revenue as a somewhat dissatisfied customer.

The main goal is to create a consistent customer experience across all touch points to exceed your and your customers' standards. By keeping an eye on the entire customer journey, you're making sure that the promise of a positive experience is kept and that you're offering superior service.

Long gone are the days when brands could buy a customer's repeat business—instead, they have to earn it with exceptional experiences and rich engagement. Now true loyalty has much more to do with overall customer experience, and far less to do with collecting points and coupons. While loyalty programs are designed to fuel transactions, today's consumers are not primarily driven by discounts, but rather by relevance."

Customers today want highly personalized communications and timely messages from brands that truly "get" them, with 91% of consumers more likely to shop with brands who recognize, remember, and provide them with personalized experiences.

Although loyalty programs may be dying, loyalty can still live on as a crucial piece of CX if brands focus on strengthening their customer relationships and offering them relevant, personalized content—and delivering it at the right time to the channels that matter most to them.

Most "loyalty" programs are misnamed, they don't generate true loyalty. Loyal customers exhibit three specific traits—they spend more, come back faster, and refer like crazy. These are all long-term behaviors.

By contrast, most companies use programs that compensate customers for taking specific actions, such as buy ten get one free cards, referral deals, and discounts for signups. But these are simply tactics while true loyalty is a strategy.

Loyalty requires a stronger connection between customer and company. When customer experience is designed with loyalty in mind, the emphasis shifts from short-term bumps to long-term gains, and from tactical to strategic. The financial benefit of great customer experience focuses on lifetime customer value. This means you must focus on having a marketing strategy designed to inspire lucrative, long-term loyalty.

2. New shoppers are more likely to turn into loyal customers.

Creating a WOW experience really impresses purchasers and ensures that they will keep doing business with you in the future. A superior experience becomes a valued and unique asset for any type of business.

Acquiring a new customer <u>costs seven times more</u> than maintaining an existing one. Investing in your existing customers will pay off and it's only a matter of time until you see positive results.

What if your customer is unhappy?

There are few things that impact a brand's reputation more than the way it responds to complaints. Customer service is an important part of developing brand loyalty, and the way you respond to unhappy consumers will determine what they say about you afterward.

Ideally, every business would rather have exclusively positive feedback, but unfortunately, that's a pretty unrealistic goal.

Service Recovery

Who are your best customers? I'll argue they're your *lost customers*. No, the winter cold hasn't frozen my brain; I left out a key phrase. Who are your best customers—*to help you with business process and product improvement?*

Every business loses customers. It's a fact of business life. And the tendency may be, especially for the small business-person, to shy away from communicating with customers who have walked away. Yet, consider what a treasure chest of information those lost customers hold. There's a reason those customers aren't buying from you. The reason may be benign. For example, they've moved or their needs have changed. But the reasons may be due to shortcomings in the way you do business or in the product or service they were buying from you. Wouldn't you like to know? Perhaps a minor correction would regain the customer. Surprisingly, a lot of companies act as if they couldn't care less why customers are defecting.

Fellow speaker and author, Janelle Barlow wrote a wonderful book with co-author Claus Moller, in 2008 by the title, *A Complaint is a Gift* (Berrett-Koehler Publishers). What an amazing mindset! What if everyone in your organization actually WELCOMED complaints?

Let me give you a personal example. Almost two years ago I purchased an espresso maker for my wife for the holidays. Being tight with a buck, I bought a refurbished unit from Overstock.com. That winter, we did a kitchen renovation so certain less critical items got boxed away, including the espresso maker. After resurfacing, we used it for another month, until the pump failed. Technically, it was out of warranty, but I felt it was reasonable to at least ask for special consideration. I wrote to the customer service manager. No response. I wrote to the Director of Customer Satisfaction directly and through the web site "contact us" feature—they would not give me the name of any senior officer. No response. I tried to email the German headquarters' customer service operation. The email on the web site didn't work. I posted the letter. No response. (I should add that Overstock.com did respond with a $20 credit although they had no compunction to do so.)

When my wife asked me last summer why I hadn't just thrown out the now dust-covered espresso maker, I opted for one last shot. I went on-line and found the name and address of the company president. I created a succinct "Customer Centric Audit" pretending my experiences were part of an audit to measure how responsive Krups was to customers. (I explained the real situation in the Epilogue.) I printed it as a professional consultant's report and sent it Priority Mail.

About two weeks later, I received a call from the customer service manager I first tried to contact. She has offered to fix or replace the machine. More interestingly, *she thanked me for the feedback*. She could not find my original letter and was surprised at the trouble I had just getting some type of response. I intend to pursue those conversations later. Last week we received the repaired machine.

How many of your customers would go this far to voice a complaint? Not many! (I justify this tenacity in the name of research, which has a germ of truth due to my business practice and academic research.) Research has shown that customers are twice as likely to voice a complaint when provided a toll-free number, and, of course, customers are most likely to complain if asked if there's a problem. Most important, customers who have had a complaint resolved effectively are more loyal than customers who have never had a complaint. That's the reason for creating service recovery programs.

Look at your own business and ask how easy you make it for customers to complain and what you do with complaint data. In other words, pretend you are a customer and do your own "customer-centric audit." Your company will fall into one of five distinct levels in complaint handling progression.

1. No response to complaints

2. Reactive response to complaints

3. Systematic response to complaints

4. Proactive complaint solicitation

5. Feedback to process or product owners for root cause correction

Note that these are cumulative. As you move through the successive stages, the customer receives some attempt at recovery, at first reactively and proactively. The company then makes it easier to hear about complaints, and finally the full value of the complaint is leveraged through operational improvement.

It seems counter intuitive to *want* to hear more complaints, but we should! We can get more complaints by letting the customer know how to voice them. Toll-free numbers and point-of-contact comment cards can work, but they're passive. Active solicitation of comments can best be done by contacting customers directly. Surveys after a completed transaction or scheduled meeting work best, depending upon the nature of your business. Today, it is important to have people who are dedicated to auditing comments about your company on social media. Responsiveness is a key to service recovery. If we wait too long, it becomes harder to resolve an issue.

The key is to let the customer know that you want their feedback—*and that you will act upon it*. That last point is key. If you don't provide service recovery and fix the underlying problem, the customer will be less likely to voice issues in the future. Also, remember to fix the problem *and* fix the customer. Included with our fixed espresso maker was a packing slip—no card or note. A small gesture could have remedied an upset customer's attitude.

Having worked with many rural hospitals in the arena of patient experience, I always make sure they have a written, and well-publicized, service recovery policy. Every employee knows what they can do to solve a patient's complaint. I go so far as to have physical "toolboxes" placed in strategic locations throughout the hospital. These toolboxes contain gift cards from $5–$25 which an employee, upon documenting the reason, can attain and present to the patient as an apology.

The key to handling negative feedback is to respond politely and assure them that you're trying your best to find a solution to their issue. Make your customer feel heard and cared for and you'll find it will pay off in the long run.

In fact, did you know that 95% of people who had a bad experience are willing to give the brand another go if they know their issue has been dealt with correctly?

3. A community of customer advocates is such a powerful tool.

Word of mouth is one of the most powerful tools a company can wish for today. The truth is, 84% of consumers do not trust advertisements or promotional emails. People are now seeking third-party validation when making an online purchase. When we book a vacation through AirBnB or VRBO, my wife insists the property have at least twenty recommendations and we read them all!

And that's why customer advocacy is so important. In light of recent digital trends, customer advocacy isn't just a smart move—it's becoming a necessity:

- Organic reach for brands on Facebook slipped 1–2%, while Instagram organic reach dropped 30% in 2020, meaning customers are becoming less likely to see the content you produce.

- 76% of Gen Xers and Millennials trust user-generated content more than branded content.

- Word of mouth marketing fuels 20–50% of all purchasing decisions.

Customer advocacy doesn't just happen by accident. Rather, it takes careful thought and an ongoing commitment from all levels of the company to prove you're worth advocating for.

1. Foster Conversations

In our current digital age, companies are breaking down corporate barriers that once prevented direct communication from consumer to brand. But companies should take it a step further by spurring two-way engagement.

People are talking about your brand, whether you realize it or not. Brands looking to build on customer advocacy must proactively step into these conversations and share responsibility in shaping a positive customer experience.

2. Promote a Customer-First Mentality

"The customer is always right" isn't just an empty motto. I grew up in retail and my Dad used to say, *"the customer is NOT always right—but they are still the customer"*! Companies who continually put the customer experience first thrive while others flounder, and they're more likely to rave about your company when you've gone the extra mile for them.

3. Personalize Your Messaging

Personalization is changing the face of marketing as we know it. It goes beyond adding a name to the subject line of an email. Rather, personalized messaging centers around creating a unique customer experience for every user.

Your customers aren't account numbers or segments of an email list. Each has unique wants, needs, and expectations of your company.

Adding personalized features like product recommendations or birthday messages, or getting a personal (not automated) response from your company can go a long way toward cementing a positive company image.

4.   Give Them Something to Believe In

Give your customers something they can believe in.

Have you wondered why the direct selling industry has grown to its current goliath state? It's not just the products. With over 18.6 million consultants and $34.9 billion in annual sales, the entire industry is based on customer advocacy.

And despite the number of consultants, these companies continue building their distribution base because they give sellers something to believe in.

Vacations, car bonuses, free products, heavy discounts, the chance to set your own schedule and quit your day job—these are driving factors behind why direct sellers advocate for their brands. They don't just sell a product; they sell a dream—a desirable vision of possibilities.

Non-direct sales companies can follow this example and instill strong beliefs, too. Don't just tell customers what a product can do—show them the full effects of how they can benefit from what you offer.

By focusing on creating amazing customer experiences and embodying the desire for your business to go above and beyond, you're creating an advocate out of every consumer.

Southwest Airlines rescues a forgotten bridesmaid dress

Imagine you just landed in Costa Rica for your sister's wedding, excited to celebrate the big day as a bridesmaid. But then you realize you forgot your bridesmaid dress back home in Texas!

That's what happened to Grayleigh Oppermann.

Understandably, she began to panic and reached out to her friends Rachel and Taylor to see if they could help her ship the dress over in time for the wedding.

First, Rachel went to FedEx but they told her they wouldn't be able to get the dress to Costa Rica before the wedding due to customs. So, she turned to Facebook. She posted in a local Facebook group to see if anyone was traveling to Costa Rica soon and could take the dress along with them. No luck there either.

As a last resort, Taylor reached out to Southwest Airlines on Twitter after seeing they had a flight to Costa Rica the next morning. She tweeted pleading for help, throwing in #WorthATry for good measure.

And it worked!

The next morning, Taylor met up with a representative from Southwest Airlines for the dress handover. From that point on, the airline kept everyone updated every step of the way. They even added a dress tracker so that Grayleigh, the bride, and everyone else could follow along:

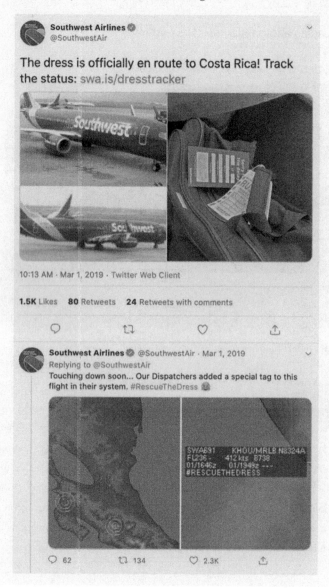

Southwest even added a special flight tag in their system—#RescueTheDress. When the flight landed, Grayleigh was finally reunited with her dress:

Southwest Airlines ✅
@SouthwestAir

Ladies and gentlemen, it has arrived.

Operation #RescueTheDress: COMPLETE!

1:10 PM · Mar 1, 2019 · Twitter for iPhone

3.4K Likes   **150** Retweets   **80** Retweets with comments

What a relief! Southwest really did save the day.

The Takeaway

The best customer experience happens across departments and works even if you have a remote support team—and this story is a great example of that. To save the day, *multiple* teams at Southwest Airlines had to be able to communicate effectively and efficiently, including the social media team, the customer service managers, the cabin crew, and the flight operators. They put communication channels and processes in place (and it helps too to have a good customer service app) to keep everyone connected, so that when something does suddenly happen, everyone is ready to go.

CRITICAL QUESTION #4

How Do We Change our Perspective?

I **ONCE HEARD** a sales trainer say, *"If you see the world through your customer's eyes, you'll see the way your customer buys."*

I LOVE THIS! It should be the mantra of every business no matter the size or scope. BUT...experience has shown me that it really takes something to see the world through the eyes of another. My experience is that it is a huge ask to experience the world as another experiences it. I find that it's all too easy to persuade oneself that one has shifted from an 'inside-out' view to an 'outside-in' view and yet be firmly stuck in that old 'inside-out' view.

What does it really take to see the world through the eyes of our customers? Allow me to share this example which I came across years ago in a wonderful book called *Infinite Vision: How Aravind Became the World's Greatest Business Case for Compassion* (BK Business) by Pavithra K. Mehta and Suchitra Shenoy (Barrett-Koehler Publishing 2011).

> While giving away free services might appear to be easy, Aravind's experience proved to the contrary. "In the early days, we didn't know better...We would go to the villages, screen patients, and tell those who needed surgery to come to the hospital for free treatment. Some showed up, but a lot of them did not. It was really puzzling to us. **Why would someone turn down the chance to see again?**" Fear, superstition, and cultural indifference can all be very real barriers to accessing medical care, but Aravind's leaders were

convinced that there was more to it than that. After a few more years and several ineffective pilots of door-to-door counseling, they arrived at the crux of the issue. "Enlightenment came when we talked to a blind beggar," ...When pressed on why he had not shown up to have his sight restored, the man replied, "You told me to come to the hospital. To do that, I would have to pay bus fare, then find money for food and medicines. **Your 'free' surgery costs me 100 rupees."**

...The research found that transport and sustenance costs, along with lost wages for oneself and accompanying family member, were daunting consideration for the rural patient. Aravind learned a valuable lesson: just because people need something you are offering for free, it does not mean they will take you up on it. **You have to make it viable for them to access your service in the context of their realities**.

Aravind Eye Hospital: It is not enough to see the world through customer eyes, your customers have to be moved to act.

So that's the first step: genuinely seeing the world through the context of the lives of your customers. And it makes no difference at all unless your organization acts on what it has learned.

What did the folks at Aravind do?

Aravind retrofitted its outreach services to address the chief barriers. In addition to the free screening at the eye camps, patients were given a free ride to one of its base hospitals, where they received surgery, accommodation, food, postoperative medication, return transport, and a follow up visit in their village, all free of charge…

"Once we did that, of course, our expenses went up…**But more importantly, our acceptance rate for surgery went up from roughly 5 percent to about 80 percent.**" For an organization aspiring to rid the world of needless blindness, this was tremendously significant….

"In hindsight, **we found two things are critical… You have to focus on the nonuser, and you have to passionately own the problem. You can address the barriers only when you own, not shift, the problems.**" Paradoxically, that mindset led to what is perhaps the most collaborative outreach system the world of eye care has ever seen.

How does your organization measure up? Do you really get how you, your offer, or your services show up for your prospective and existing customers? Do you really understand how your customers experience your organization across the customer journey? Is your leadership committed to doing what it takes to make it easy for prospects to buy from you? How easy is it for customers to keep doing business with you? Is your organization up for passionately owning the problem or is it designed to hide and/or shift the problems on to customers and others? These are crucial questions to ask yourself if we are to see the world through our customers' eyes.

Have you ever gone shopping for new shoes, clothing, electronics or whatever—and come across a product that is exactly right? The features you need, in the design that works best for you? That suddenly becomes a "must have" purchase for you—and the price isn't much of a factor.

It's not a coincidence. Manufacturers put a lot of effort into consumer research and testing—focus groups and other ways to find out what customers are looking for. Their purpose is to create a product that will appeal to the customers they want to reach.

As a businessperson, that should be your purpose too—**to understand your prospective clients so well that you can design a service offering that becomes a "must have" purchase for them.**

That's why, in your own work, you're more likely to win the work if you show that your service for your clients is tailor-made to fit their needs. You may even be able to charge a higher price for your services, just as you're probably willing to pay more for a product that absolutely delights you.

I saw this approach recently in my quest for a solution about apples—the fruit not the tech company! I want to bring more local food into my own diet (mostly, to reduce my carbon footprint). That implies more apple-intensive recipes—apples being about the only fresh fruit available year-round from local sources in my often-frozen state.

But peeling, coring, and chopping a dozen apples can be a pain. So, I looked online, and found a device that provides a pain-free solution. It looks like a cross between a miniature carpentry lathe and a nineteenth-century kitchen device. I bought it, and it rocks!

The design of this device holds a few useful business lessons, which can point you toward developing products, services, and offerings for your customer.

The designers of my apple-solution device must have known that most people planning to buy something are actually looking for a way to solve a problem, as I was. They realized that most bakers don't want to just get the core out of the apple. They want to solve a problem, which is how to get the apples into a form that can go into an apple pie. This means that they need something that will core the apple, but also peel and slice it.

So, the designers produced a gizmo that does all three. It cores, peels and slices. The apples slide out of it in a tidy white spiral that I can chop into quarters with two knife strokes and drop into the baking dish. It fits the need.

BUT...the designers also realized that bakers need options. Some people want the skin left on the apple, and not every recipe calls for apples that have been sliced (like, baked apples). So, the device can be adjusted to leave the skin on the apple, and also so that it doesn't slice the apple. That's thinking with the end purpose of the customer in mind. It's a solution to a problem, not just a piece of hardware.

You, too, need to design your service offering so it's a solution to a problem, rather than just a series of functions you perform. To do this, take a step back from thinking of it as you are selling your services to your clients. Consider the issues your clients are facing, and how your work helps them deal with those issues.

The designers of my apple gizmo looked at the world through a baker's eyes, and it helped them design a product that met a range of needs. That's why you need to grow your ability to look at the world through your clients' eyes.

I saw this recently when working with a PhD employed by one of my clients. Janice (as I'll call her) specializes in the narrow field of remote sensing—in her case, analyzing the images taken from satellites. She uses images taken with satellite-based LIDAR (like radar, only using light instead of radio waves) to determine whether there have been changes in the earth's topography.

To me, that sounded really, really geeky. But interestingly, in a geeky way, this PhD was clearly in love with her work. That came through in what I can only describe as the sparkle in her voice. I asked Janice how her remote-sensing skills are applied. She told me that much of her work was for the mining industry. The tunnels of abandoned underground mines sometimes collapse, she explained, and this can cause subsidence of the surface topography above, or even sinkholes.

That's a bad thing, because it can cause changes to watercourses and even entire drainage basins, which is an environmental violation. Collapses and subsidence can also harm foundations of buildings, roadways, railroads, airports, and other surface installations, which can result in lawsuits.

Janice told me that before satellite-based LIDAR, the only way to determine subsidence was from the ground—crews of surveyors walking over a site, measuring topography changes with theodolites and other survey instruments. It was slow, painstaking work that was hard to do with accuracy when there was snow on the ground. This meant that mining companies tended to not commission subsidence surveys all that often, and those that they did commission could only be done at certain times of the year.

So, I asked Janice what her work did to help her mining company clients achieve their business goals. There was a pause at the other end of the phone line. I could almost hear the wheels turning inside her brilliant brain. She had, despite her evident intelligence, not thought much about what business purpose there was for the work she was doing.

Then she came out with an answer: "I can help mining companies get their survey results faster, so they can find areas where underground workings are collapsing," she said. I asked what this meant for the mining companies. "It means that they can take action early, and backfill the mine workings to support them, while the problem is still manageable."

I find this really common in mid-career technical people. They put all their focus on being technically watertight—producing reliable, accurate findings. And that's a good thing. But sometimes it means that they lose focus on the purpose of their work, which is generally to solve a business problem, or access an opportunity.

To sum up: My client, who had a strong technical twist to their work, thought that their client was buying *really great science*. Accurate, elegant, maybe even pushes the technical envelope a bit. BUT…clients aren't buying *really great science*. **They're buying a disappeared problem**. Patrons don't buy from you because you have a great service or product, but to solve a business problem.

Someone once said, "*I would like to travel the world with you twice. Once to see the world. Twice to see the world the way you see the world.*"

See your company, your services, and your products from your customers eyes and it will begin to change the way you offer your end-to-end experience.

On a sticky July evening, the multimillion-album-selling vocal group One Direction (AKA 1D) made a stop at the Izod Center in East Rutherford, NJ, on its international "Take Me Home" tour.

The capacity crowd of 19,000+ fans, composed primarily of frenzied 9- to 16-year-old Jersey girls, welcomed the young UK stars with screams and open arms.

For those unfamiliar with the worldwide pop cultural impact of 1D, here's a quick summary:

The group's five members were originally contestants on the British version of "The X Factor" in 2010. They were signed to Simon Cowell's Syco Records (marketed and distributed worldwide by Columbia Records).

Their first album, "Up All Night," was released in 2012, and their second album, "Take Me Home," came out in 2013. The group has sold 19 million singles and 10 million albums around the world.

Tickets for their tours have sold out within minutes. The band itself has since disbanded but, because my daughter was a huge fan and in the interest of doing research (!) I go on...

The passionate, emotional enthusiasm (and sizable financial expenditures) that 1D inspired among its massive global fan base was not a fluke: It was the result of a meticulously nurtured loyalty-building strategy that was on full display at the Izod Center that night.

Companies that wish to develop positive connections with their own customers would be wise to learn from 1D's examples, which were carefully planned by their managers and flawlessly choreographed by the producers of their "Take Me Home" tour.

1. Deliver outstanding quality

One would expect 1D to put on an adequate show that pleased its young fans. But what happened at the Izod Center was a powerful spectacle that truly wowed the *Directioners*; the term for a **super** fan **of the British/Irish boy band.**

Laser light effects. Explosions. Smoke. Confetti and streamers. Dazzling graphics and colorful, fast-paced videos on a wide, two-story screen behind 1D and the band. All were coordinated and displayed tastefully and impressively.

The Takeaway

Every element of 1D's concert was calculated to dazzle its young fans/customers, and they all worked. Companies should aim to achieve such excellence in every aspect of their customer interactions by...

- Creating and delivering a first-rate product or service

- Providing courteous customer care

- Nurturing valuable dialogues and helpful social media interactions

- Crafting user-friendly multimedia sales and marketing collateral

2. Understand your customers' NGDs

The overriding NGD (need/goal/desire) for the majority of the Izod Center audience was to get closer than they had ever been before to their favorite 1D member (or, in the words of the young Directioners, to *"breathe the same air as 1D").*

One Direction served up the goods. Each member was featured, spotlighted, and called out throughout the show, giving their respective admirers plenty to shriek about.

And, in what was a smart move, the guys were attired in hip yet informal outfits: They didn't wear the glittery suits or elaborate costumes that boy bands of yore (e.g., Backstreet Boys, N' Sync, New Kids On The Block) sported when performing. This choice made the group's members more accessible (and attainable) to the shrieking tweens/teens.

The Takeaway

One Direction's management and concert producers didn't create a concert experience that they thought would reflect their target consumers' NGDs; they created a concert experience that they knew would reflect their target consumers' NGDs.

Whether it was by research, observation, experience, or a combination of the three, the teams behind 1D's show succeeded because they had an accurate appreciation of what Directioners wished to derive from the group's live presentation.

Companies should take this same approach when researching their own customers' specific NGDs. Rather than assuming or guessing, companies should instead aim to learn exactly what the NGDs are and then reflect those in the product/service.

3. Create real connections with your customers

One Direction bonded with Izod Center fans in three noteworthy ways.

First, midway through the concert, the guys took a break from the music and invited the audience to send them tweets with questions about their tour. The fans' queries ("What's your favorite American food/TV show/etc.?") were posted on two massive video screens on either side of the main stage at the front of the arena.

After answering each tweeted question, the group then gave a shout-out to—and had a spotlight shined on—the section of the arena from which the question originated, sending the fans who were seated in that section into joyous hysterics.

Second, in sing-alongs and the call/response parts of songs that it performed throughout the night, 1D let the Jersey crowd know that they were the loudest and most enthusiastic audience on the tour. That incredible news made the arena's decibel level explode into the ear-bleed zone.

(I made the mistake of telling my daughter that 1D probably says the same thing to the audiences at each of its concerts, but she firmly insisted that 1D "would never do that"...)

Third, at numerous times throughout the evening, 1D members thanked the Directioners for coming to the show, and let them know that the group would never have attained its current level of success—or had a chance to perform in New Jersey—if the fans hadn't been so supportive of their music and careers.

The Takeaway

In each of the above examples, One Direction used the concert to establish powerful, memorable, and direct relationships with fans/customers. 1D also expressed tremendous gratitude to fans for the group's achievements.

Using social media channels, customer service channels (phone, chat, email), and email marketing efforts, companies should seek to creatively connect and interact with their own customers, as well as devise sincere ways to express their thanks for customers' support (i.e., purchases). Implemented correctly and genuinely, a company's multi-dimensional relationship-building efforts can yield significant customer loyalty, improved marketplace image, and future sales.

4. Exceed your customers' expectations, then exceed them again

If One Direction had put on an energetic performance of fans' favorite songs, interacted with the audience, and enhanced the show with dynamic videos and explosive effects, the Directioners would have gone home very satisfied.

1D did that—and did so one better.

Just before the show's halfway mark, the group ascended stairs that led to a high platform above the floor of their stage. Each member attached a waist cable to his microphone stand. The elevated platform, which was tethered to an elaborate track apparatus that was bolted into the ceiling, began to slowly move from the front of the arena to the back—where it lowered the guys onto a second stage.

As the platform journeyed across the length of the Izod Center, the screams from the rear of the arena increased in volume. Fans in the faraway sections who were able to make out their favorite 1D members only via binoculars or on the giant video screens, were now closer to them than they could ever have imagined—or their seat locations suggested—they'd be.

Without doubt, that significant phone memory within the Izod Center was filled to capacity with photos and videos of this unexpected crowd-thrilling surprise.

The Takeaway

To survive in the marketplace and keep up with your competitors, deliver what your customers expect. But to thrive in the marketplace and dominate your competitors, deliver more than what your customers expect. Deliver WOW, surprise and delight!

5. Surprise and innovate

A mom I spoke to said that she had heard 1D's albums played in their entirety by her daughter hundreds of times over the past year and that she knew all of the songs that the group sang at the show. One song, however, was unfamiliar.

Toward the end of the concert, One Direction performed a guitar-heavy, alternative rock-sounding song called "Teenage Dirtbag." The Mom figured that she might have missed it when her daughter was listening to her albums, or maybe it had been released as an overseas single and hadn't been included on 1D's American releases. She asked her daughter when 1D had put the song out, and she didn't know. In fact, she had never heard 1D sing it before.

That "Teenage Dirtbag" was new to the young girl—and all of the Directioners at the Izod Center—didn't seem to matter: By the end of the second chorus, everyone was singing along. Elaborate graphics on the Izod Center video screens featuring the song's lyrics and 1D as comic book action heroes pretty much made the song theirs.

It turns out that "Teenage Dirtbag" was an alt-rock hit in 2000 by the band Wheatus. According to Billboard magazine, "Teenage Dirtbag" offered "keen melody, inventive production, and cool lyric about those who have felt like underlings during high school." Billboard went on to say that it "stands strongly on its own as an emphatic anthem and a song many teens will be proud to push hard from their car speakers."

The Takeaway

1D's decision to create a version of "Teenage Dirtbag" was risky, unexpected, and absolutely brilliant. Whether it was a tease of its new album's sound, or a messaging tie-in with its anti-bullying partnership with Office Depot, or just something cool to perform live, "Teenage Dirtbag" was executed flawlessly—and the group's fans/customers loved it.

Companies should strategically embrace similar boldness and innovation to surprise their customers and the marketplace. It's easy to coast when a successful formula is discovered. It takes guts and a long-term perspective to intelligently expand on that formula in a way that will please current customers and attract prospects.

One Direction's success is no accident. It's the well-planned result of the band's charisma and talent combined with excellent songwriting/production, spectacular marketing, and—perhaps most important—an impeccable customer experience.

CRITICAL QUESTION #5

How Do I Get My People More Engaged?

AS BOTH A business professional and consumer you know that bad experiences often stay with a customer longer than a positive one. It's for this reason a poor experience with your business can ruin a relationship with a customer for good.

In fact, a recent survey found that 95% of customers were likely to share a bad experience with a brand compared to 87% who said they were likely to share a good experience.

By understanding and paying close attention to all of your customer touch points however, you can get a high-level view of the quality of your customer service and ensure your staff continually provides the best service possible.

But, here is the key to understanding touch points. Remember we said previously that only 33% of American workers are engaged at what they do in the workplace according to the report, "State of the American Workplace"? Touch points (and the exercise included in this chapter) will absolutely get your people more engaged every day.

You see, I believe that engagement comes from the front line up, NOT from management down. By having your people identify THEIR touch points, take ownership, and commit to making small changes in those touch points, you can completely change the experience.

The more engaged your people are INTERNALLY, the better the experience EXTERNALLY!

What is a Customer Touch Point?

Before we can discuss providing customer service at each touch point, it's important to first identify what a customer touchpoint is.

I defined touch point previously as **any opportunity you have to INFLUENCE the customer experience**. This can occur at any time in the buying process from ads before they make a purchase to shopping in your physical or online store to a follow up survey after their treatment in a hospital. These customer touch points are opportunities to offer your customers WOW, surprise, and delight, turning them into a repeat customer, and more likely to recommend your business to others. However, a negative experience at any given touch point can cause you to get a negative review, lose a customer, or both.

Not only does a good customer experience help you keep customers, but it also encourages customers to spend more.

85% of buyers have said they are willing to pay more simply because they had a great customer experience.

The bottom line—businesses simply cannot afford not to provide their customers with great customer service at each touch point. Accumulatively, all of those great service touch points will add up to an incredible customer experience.

How to Identify Your Customer Touchpoints

Now that you understand what a customer touch point is, it's time to identify them. Understanding what your customer/patient/member touch points are will enable you to provide a memorable customer experience and make better overall business decisions. Furthermore, once you are able to identify what creates loyalty to your brand, you'll be able to drive more brand loyalty.

To identify customer touch points you need to consider all the ways a customer can encounter your business, starting with before they've even heard about your brand.

Common customer touch points may include:

- Ads

- Business directories

- Customer reviews

- Word of mouth

- Your website

- Scheduling apps or calendars

- Social media

- Product catalogs

- Your physical store (or office)

- Your customer service department

- Employee interaction

- Emails (promotional or transactional)

- Purchase follow-ups

- Your telephone system

- The check-out process

When it comes to your business, your customer touch points may include some or all of these, or even some that are not on this list.

Remember—the definition of a touch point is *any opportunity you have to INFLUENCE the customer experience.*

While they do not necessarily require a customer to interact with your brand, in most cases they will. For example, seeing how you interact with other customers or on social media can have an impact on customers you aren't dealing with directly.

When identifying these touch points with your team it's important not to be vague. Simply saying "online" is not enough of an identifier to qualify as a touch point. Google Ads or your website's chat feature, however, is considered a touch point. Also, be careful not to fall into the trap of only looking at marketing touch points. If I am waiting to go into my dentist's office and need to use the men's room and it's dirty, that is a touch point. Think broadly when identifying touch points.

To identify your touch points you need to understand your business from your customer's point of view. What happens when you search for your business? What is the first point of contact they have with your brand—is it your website? If so, does your homepage clearly identify how you can help or what you offer? If they click on your online chat—is it working properly? If you offer a subscription service, how easy it is to cancel their membership? All of these questions will help you dive deeper into your business and understand how your customers see and experience your brand.

Understanding How to Utilize Customer Touch Points

Now that you understand what a customer touch point is, and have identified the touch points for your brand, you need to actively improve them. For example, if you tested out the chat feature on your website and find that it's faulty, research a better version. Understanding how to leverage live chat is especially important if this is one of your customer touch points.

Touch Point Exercise

EXERCISE LOGISTICS

(You will require a flip chart with paper and markers—red and black are ideal. I suggest that you facilitate but have someone else to write on the flip chart.)

1) Make sure that everyone understands the meaning for touch point: *"Any opportunity you have to INFLUENCE the customer experience."*

Give them some examples:

    (a) if someone comes to our office and they can't find a parking spot = TOUCH POINT!

    (b) a guest uses the restroom and it's dirty = TOUCH POINT!

    (c) a business card we hand to someone = TOUCH POINT!

    (d) an invoice we mail to a client = TOUCH POINT!

2) Ask everyone to tell you the touch points of the organization or team (whichever is more appropriate), and have your helper start writing every one of them on the flip chart. When you run out of paper, have your 'scribe' tear it off and tape it to the wall and keep going on a fresh piece of paper.

    At first, it will be like pulling teeth to get answers, but as people start to understand, you will develop dozens of touch points. Allow everyone to contribute. You should have multiple papers up on the walls when all contributions are exhausted.

3) Advise the group that you are now going to take a break (you decide for how long) and tell them that there are (RED) markers up at the front and that everyone is on the honor system. During the break, they are to come up and put FIVE (5) red checks beside the FIVE top priority touch points (in THEIR opinion) for the team/organization. Also clarify that they must put only ONE check beside any one item to encourage them NOT to put all five checks beside one.

4) When you return from the break, determine the top five by the number of red checks and point them out to the group (circle them or underline them).

5) Make it clear that THEY have identified these five. It doesn't come from management or anywhere else. Ask them how the team/organization can tweak just these five touch points to make them better. Write the suggestions on a new piece of flip chart paper.

6) Finally, ask for input on two things:

Who is going to OWN/CHAMPION this touch point and a time commitment as to when the change will occur.

This will get buy-in from everyone at a grassroots level and people will be more engaged at making them work. As an addendum to the exercise, every time a touch point is made better, go back to the original list and have the team pick the NEXT priority and go through the same steps.

By constantly tweaking our touch points, the external customer experience gets better and better.

Keep in mind this isn't a one-time practice. As technology and customer needs evolve, you need to continually monitor your touch points to ensure they are remaining effective.

It's also important to ensure your staff has the skills needed to provide quality customer service at each touch point. Do they understand active listening to ensure a customer's needs are being met? Are there protocols in place to follow-up with a customer after they have reached out to you?

This is a great opportunity to improve your business' customer strategy. For example, this exercise may cause you to realize your approach to customer service isn't as personal as you had previously thought. Armed with this information, you can take steps to create a more personalized experience for your customers. After all, **76% of customers have reported they expect brands to understand both their needs and expectations.**

> *"Your brand is a story unfolding across all customer touch points"*
> — *Jordan Sachs*

If you're still unsure of your customer touch points or their effectiveness, you can also take this opportunity to understand your customers better by completing a Customer Journey Map. Keep reading to find out more!

CRITICAL QUESTION #6

How Can We Understand Our Customer
Better?

WHEN YOU THINK of your customer, who comes to mind?

Can you name their intentions, motivations, and pain points? Better yet, do you know why they are choosing *your* company or hospital or association among competitors?

Defining customer needs, problems, and interactions with your company may seem overwhelming and at times, unnecessary. However, understanding every customer's experience at each stage of the customer journey is crucial for turning business insights into long-term improvement strategies.

Creating a customer journey map can help you and your company visualize how customers feel at all brand touch points so you can avoid potential issues ahead of time, increase customer retention, and discover key information to make the best decisions for your business. Depending on the size of your organization, you may get everyone involved in creating your map OR you can do this by department as well.

What is a customer journey map?

A customer journey map is a visual storyline of every engagement your customer has with your service, brand, or product. The creation of a journey map puts you directly in the mind of the consumer, so you can see where you may be missing the mark, what you are doing right, and where you can make improvements across the customer lifecycle.

Retail customer journey

A journey map lays out all touch points that your customer may have with your brand—from how they first heard of you through social media or brand advertising, to their direct interactions with your product, website, or support team—and includes all of the actions your customer takes to complete an objective across a period of time.

Using a customer journey map to improve the customer experience

Outlining your current processes helps to visualize what the customer is experiencing in real time and may unveil common pain points that need to be addressed. Through this exercise, you'll also be able to connect with your buyer and in turn, influence your organization to prioritize the customer experience (CX) through shared understanding.

Gaining a deeper understanding of your customer

> *"Experience maps look at a broader context of human behavior. They show how the organization fits into a person's life."*
>
> — *Jim Kalbach, author of Mapping Experiences*

How does your customer feel when they can't get in touch with customer service on an issue they're experiencing? Or, if their package doesn't arrive on time?

You may be imagining a situation where those instances happened to you outside of the workplace and can remember feelings of frustration. You assume this customer may feel the same and can relate to their sentiment. The ability to establish empathy for your customers and identify how they're feeling at every turn is what makes customer journey mapping a powerful exercise.

A customer journey map expands that empathy on a broader level so you have a true understanding of their experience and can be meaningful in your organization's customer experience improvement strategies.

Your map can help answer questions such as:

- Is my online interface user-friendly and matching customer expectations? Why is the user navigating away from the site so quickly?

- How often is my customer reaching out to customer service and is the team able to address the issues in a timely manner?

- How is the customer interacting with my brand before they decide to make a purchase? How are they feeling at this stage?

Understanding the customer from an empathetic, bird's-eye view means having a deeper insight into their needs at every touch point so you can improve CX processes to meet their expectations.

Creating a customer-centric company

Aligning toward the same company objectives is essential for strategic customer experience goal planning and success tracking. When you create a journey map, you have a customer-centered tool to refer to and distribute across the company.

With your customer journey map, you can:

- Use your map to train team members on CX standards and best practices

- Present the visual diagram in company-wide meetings to map out customer-focused quarterly goals

- Include the sales team in your map assessment to improve onboarding flows

- Review the map with your customer service team to strategize how to reduce obstacles throughout the customer lifecycle

Using visual mapping to tell a story to your company will not only set a united standard for exceptional customer care, but it will improve customer experience and customer retention in the long run.

Customer journey map design

There's no correct or incorrect way to create a customer journey map. However, before you begin, consider aligning your map with a chosen customer persona and think through which journeys and stages make the most sense for your business to measure.

Creating a customer persona

A customer persona is a fictional character that represents your average customer based on user and market research. Imagining this persona's age, job function, personal goals, etc. can help you step into the customer's shoes and thoroughly develop the customer journey story. Have some fun with this and be creative but accurate.

Start by creating three personas at most to help in narrowing your character and design focus.

Deciding what to measure

Next, you will need to decide what you want to measure and what goal you're trying to achieve.

Perhaps you want to revisit current customer success processes or take a closer look at your prospect's experience through the selling timeline. Whatever you choose, your customer journey map is customizable and should evolve over time to meet your business needs.

Organizing with touch points and stages

As you begin your customer journey design, you may want to organize your map with touch points and stages:

B2B customer journey

- **Identify touch points**: Remember, a touch point is any opportunity you have to influence the customer experience. (See the previous chapter on touch points for more detailed information.) From advertisements, to a thank you note they receive after a purchase, consider including these touch points within your map so you can collect feedback and identify patterns on how they're feeling at each interaction.

- **Write out the stages**: Every time your customer engages with your brand, there is a goal-driven action behind it. Break down the customer journey in stages (or phases) based on the customer's need throughout their journey.

Mapping out personas and defining specific customer touch points can seem time-consuming. Use Excel documents to organize your map, or work from customer journey templates you can find for free online, to set a simple foundation for your diagram creation process.

Using survey data to boost your customer journey map

Research is crucial to finding out your customer's motivations, roadblocks, continued pain points, and successes. If you don't have the survey data to answer these questions, you could be building your map from assumptions, leaving room for misguided strategic planning down the line.

B2B customer journey and survey examples

DELIGHTED CES
We made it easy
for you to compare
solutions.

DELIGHTED CSAT
How satisfied were
you with the contract
process?

DELIGHTED CSAT
How satisfied were you
with your onboarding
experience?

DELIGHTED NPS
How likely are you to
recommend our brand
to your peers?

I need a solution to meet my business needs. → Research options → Decision/ sign a contract → Onboarding → Ongoing usage → Support → Renewal

DELIGHTED CSAT
How satisfied were you
with the training your
team received?

DELIGHTED NPS
How likely are you to
recommend this solution
to your peers?

DELIGHTED CES
The support rep made it
easy to solve my issues.

Source: Bain & Company

Consider using Net Promoter Score (NPS), Customer Satisfaction (CSAT), or Customer Effort Score (CES) surveys to capture first-hand customer feedback to include within your customer journey map. Then, choose between a variety of surveying channels (Email, SMS, Web, Link, etc.) to reach your audience wherever they are.

Here are some question examples to include in your survey:

- [CSAT]: How satisfied were you with your onboarding experience?

- [CSAT]: How satisfied were you with our checkout process?

- [NPS]: How likely are you to recommend this solution to your peers?

- [NPS]: How likely are you to recommend this store to your friends or family?

- [CES]: The website made it easy for me to compare options

- [CES]: The support reps made it easy to get my questions answered

After you select your survey, questions, and channel, specify when and how often surveys are triggered throughout the customer lifecycle. Before you know it, your customer journey map includes up-to-date feedback for you to start analyzing and acting on CX feedback regularly.

Customer journey mapping is not a one-time exercise. Once you're finished with the basics, don't forget to observe and analyze feedback and results. Based on that, make sure you do the necessary tweaks in your customer journey map. This is the only way you can ensure your customers always have an awesome experience when interacting with your company.

CRITICAL QUESTION #7

What Can Our Customer Tell Us?

EVERY PRODUCT OR service is made for its customers. It's created to either solve their problems or fulfill their needs. Your product or service revolves around your customers and their experiences, and every single day, you're making significant efforts to provide them with a positive experience.

This journey of providing your customers with a positive experience starts from the moment they land on your website and extends beyond the moment they become your customer. Although it's a never-ending commitment, encouraging them to become a loyal customer by retaining them is definitely considered a milestone of growth.

Many of you have heard me say, *"Customer experience is the new marketing."* And that couldn't be truer today.

Your customers' opinions and feedback are one of the most essential components for the sustainability and growth of your business and are considered important throughout the customer lifecycle. So, why don't we involve them enough? Because we don't know how to.

How do you know if the customer is happy? Or dissatisfied? How do you decide to work on a new feature, if you don't even know whether the customer needs it or not? What do you think your customers expect from you? Did they find what they're looking for?

A customer's experience and feedback should be the only factors that validate important decisions within your business.

In this chapter we'll dig into customer experience survey questions and real survey examples—as well as what makes them so impactful.

Customer Satisfaction Survey Questions

If you want to obtain valuable feedback from your customers, then you have to be asking them the right questions. Sharing information isn't always an easy task, and it's not the customer's job to provide your business with constructive criticism. Instead, it's the surveyor's responsibility to create a thought-provoking prompt that engages the participant.

If you're getting stuck on deciding what to ask your customers, here are some of the types of questions we recommend including on your customer experience survey:

Product Usage

When it comes to customer success and satisfaction, it's critical that your business collects feedback about your product or service. If you don't, then it's more difficult to assess customer needs and provide effective solutions. Finding out how satisfied your users are with your offer provides your marketing and product teams with valuable information that can be used to improve customer loyalty and retention.

Some questions that you could ask in this section are:

1. How often do you use the product or service?

2. Does the product help you achieve your goals?

3. What is your favorite tool or portion of the product or service?

4. What would you improve if you could?

Demographics

Demographics are essential to marketing and sales teams because they make it easier for companies to segment customers into buyer personas. By grouping customers together based on key characteristics, this categorization helps employees visualize their target audience. Marketing and sales teams can then use that information to pursue leads that are most likely to convert. Here are some demographics questions that you should consider including in your next survey:

1. How old are you?

2. Where are you located?

3. If applicable, what gender do you identify as?

4. What is your employment status?

5. What is your marital status and do you have children?

When asking these types of questions, be sure to embrace a proactive and inclusive approach. These questions shouldn't be mandatory, so always provide an option for customers to omit an answer. Your goal is to extract honest information, but you don't want it to come at the expense of the customer's comfort.

Satisfaction Scale

Sometimes there are aspects of your offer or business that you want feedback on, but they aren't things that your customers are actively addressing. In these cases, it helps to be direct with your customers and ask them how they feel about these specific details. Before you do though, you'll have to determine a quantifiable way to measure their responses. Adopting a satisfaction scale section is a great way to create a consistent approach to quantifying this subjective survey feedback. A few ways that you can implement this scale are:

1. A scale measuring from 1 to 10 (or another number). 1 is an extremely unsatisfied opinion and 10 meaning the customer was very satisfied.

2. A descriptive scale that measures a customer's response from unsatisfied to satisfied. The customer is a given a short list of responses to choose from that range from "very unsatisfied" to "very satisfied."

3. A picture scale that uses images to symbolize customer satisfaction. For example, you can use happy, sad, and indifferent emojis to quickly communicate customer feedback.

Open-Text

Open-text questions are survey questions that allow the participant to write out their response within a text box. This allows users to fully express their opinions using the customer's voice instead of the company's pre-written responses. While they can sometimes be time-consuming to analyze, these questions encourage the participant to be honest and give them the freedom to address any topic. Open-text questions can be an instrumental asset when determining the core values of your customers. Here are open-text questions you can ask in your next survey:

1. In your own words, describe how you feel about (insert company name or product here).

2. How can we improve your experience with the company?

3. What's working for you and why?

4. What can our employees do better?

5. Do you have any additional comments or feedback for us?

Longevity

In the last section of your survey, you'll want to include questions about the steps that will happen after submission. These questions permit your team to follow up with the participant in the future. This comes in handy when you roll out changes and want to get updated feedback from the same customers that were surveyed earlier. You can phrase these types of questions in a few different ways:

1. May we contact you to follow up on these responses?

2. In the future, would you be willing to take this survey again?

3. If we were to update (insert product feature here), could we reach back out to talk about these changes?

While measuring customer satisfaction can be tricky to manage, asking effective questions can reveal highly valuable customer insights. As I've established, measuring customer satisfaction means taking multiple factors into account. You'll need to be creative to stay relevant and unobtrusive, and draw pertinent conclusions from the mass of information you collect. No metric is perfect on its own, and the real measure of your customers' satisfaction lies at the intersection of your collected data and your customers' emotions.

How Starbucks Used Their Suggestion Program to Give Their Customers a Voice

If I thought that Starbucks needed to start making a Mocha Caramel Coconut Java Chip Frappucino, I could simply submit my idea at MyStarbucksIdea. com. This is a form of asking your customer for feedback.

The coffee giant launched MyStarbucksIdea.com, an online suggestion box, in 2008.

The site gives customers an opportunity to submit their ideas and feedback to Starbucks. People can share ideas, vote on them, and discuss them.

Starbucks chief information officer Chris Bruzzo hoped that a few hundred ideas would trickle into the site in the first few days after the site went live. However, about 300 suggestions were submitted within the first hour and more than 100,000 votes had been cast by the end of the week.

What makes MyStarbucksIdea successful is that Starbucks is actively paying attention to it and actually listening to their customers' ideas.

Great customer ideas don't just sit in the system; featured Starbucks Idea Partners actively look through ideas, implement them, and let customers know that they're implementing them.

From 2008–2013, more than 150,000 ideas were submitted and 277 had been implemented.

The green drink stoppers (or splash sticks) that keep hot coffee from splashing onto you, free Wi-Fi access, mocha coconut frappucinos, hazelnut macchiatos, and cake pops are all available thanks to customers who submitted the ideas on MyStarbucksIdea.com. You can take a look at all ideas launched in the MyStarbucksIdea blog.

Starbucks values and understands their customers ideas. The same goes for any organization. Your employees, in addition to your customers, have first-hand experience on what needs to be improved.

CRITICAL QUESTION #8

How Do We Measure Customer Experience?

MANY OF OUR clients have no Key Performance Indicators (KPIs) by which to measure customer experience. As I have mentioned in other chapters, there are five areas of concentration on which EVERY organization of ANY size should focus. These KPIs are ones on which every employee at every level can become a cheerleader.

They are, in no specific order,

1. Net Promoter Score

2. Employee Engagement Survey Scores

3. Total Sales Growth

4. Customer Retention

5. Employee Retention

Net Promoter Score

> *"High performing organizations which focus on CX, have Net Promoter Scores TWO TIMES higher than the average company."*
>
> *— Gary Simpson, author*

Asking the ultimate question allows companies to track promoters and detractors, producing a clear measure of an organization's performance through its customers' eyes, its Net Promoter Score.

To calculate NPS, start with the ultimate question, *"How likely are you to recommend us to a friend or colleague?"* and score the answers on a zero-to-ten scale. Your Net Promoter Score is simply the percentage of customers who are promoters (those who scored 9 or 10) minus the percentage who are detractors (those who scored 0 to 6).

The Net Promoter System was developed in 2002 by Fred Reichheld, a Bain & Company consultant, out of the need for a customer experience metric that is predictive of customer loyalty and business growth.

After scrutinizing how traditional customer satisfaction survey questions correlate to consumer behavior, Reichheld concluded that evaluating customer loyalty versus customer churn was the answer. The carefully phrased NPS question, "How likely are you to recommend [company] to a friend?" has since been adopted by top brands worldwide.

A customer that is willing to recommend (promote) your company is also more likely to stick with you for the long haul. However, a customer that rates you poorly is more likely to detract from your business by churning or spreading negative word of mouth. NPS helps you identify both types of customers so you can improve your business.

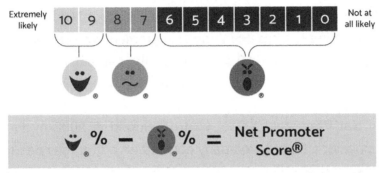

How likely is it you would recommend us to a friend?

Source: Bain & Company

How the Scoring Works

Score the answers to the ultimate question on a simple zero-to-ten scale. This scale is familiar and easy for customers to understand. And the responses tend to cluster in three groups, each one characterized by different attitudes, and more importantly, different behaviors linked to economic value.

Although there are many NPS question variations, the NPS methodology for improving the customer experience follows four basic steps:

STEP ONE

Ask the question

NPS is comprised of a carefully crafted single question survey. Customers answer this question in two parts. The first part is a 0–10 numerical rating. This provides a standardized quantitative benchmark that can be tracked over time.

Open-ended feedback

The second half of the NPS survey is a free-form follow-up question. This is where the real power of NPS reveals itself. It allows the customer to provide context for their rating in their own words, free from any bias that targeted survey questions might impart. For example, it might simply read, *"Tell us more about why you gave us the number you gave."*

One warning I give clients is that you have to read this second response carefully. If a customer indicates that they gave you an '8' because *"I never give higher than 8 to anyone"* then they are actually a promoter of your business even though a score of 8 would label them as 'Passive.'

Deliver the survey

Your NPS survey can be distributed through a variety of methods—email, text, or even in person. Most companies find it helpful to have a dedicated NPS tool to deliver the survey automatically after the customer has had a full experience of the brand. NPS platforms also help tally the responses and calculate your score. You can also use online tools like SurveyMonkey, JotForm, or SurveyGizmo.

STEP TWO

Group the responses

Customers are segmented into three groups according to their numerical response to the 0–10 rating question. But what do the different groupings actually mean?

PROMOTER (Score of 9 or 10)

"I really love your product. It's exactly what I have been looking for!"

A promoter will go out of their way to recommend your product or service, often unprompted. They are willing to put their personal reputation on the line for it.

PASSIVE (Score of 7 or 8)

"It's pretty good. I had a few issues here and there, but it got the job done."

A passive probably liked your product or service, but it wasn't a slam dunk. They may mention it in the right context, but they are unlikely to personally vouch for it.

DETRACTOR (Score of 6 or below)

"I wasn't able to get it to work. I tried for hours. This is so frustrating!"

A detractor will proactively take any opportunity to dissuade people from using your product or service. They often speak louder than promoters.

STEP THREE

Calculate your NPS

NPS provides a score, ranging from -100 to +100, that serves as a report card, grading your overall customer experience.

So, as an example, a recent client found that 71% of their customers are promoters and 14% are detractors.

The NPS formula

Their NPS numerical score is the percentage of promoters **minus** the percentage of detractors.

$$71 - 14 = \boxed{57}$$

If you already have responses from a previous NPS survey, you can calculate your NPS with an interactive NPS calculator or benchmark your NPS scores against others in your industry. You can find many online resources to do this.

STEP FOUR

Track your NPS over time

Your numerical NPS allows you to quantify how changes you make to your product affect the customer experience over time.

Single value charts can clearly summarize an NPS Score. You could also use these to show counts or percentages of Promoters, Passives, and Detractors within the NPS score.

NPS Last 3 Months
11

Detractor %	Passives %	Promoter %
25	**38**	**37**

Seeing the breakdown of the categories with NPS lets you focus on which group you want to target to increase your company or product's rating.

Stacked bar charts are popular because they visualize the three groups that compose NPS. The group breakdown can be shown as total or percentage. However, it can be hard to determine the NPS and differentiate between groups if they are close in size.

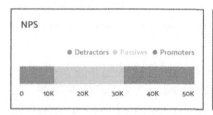
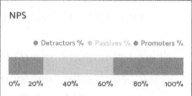

Alternatively, we can create the plot with a 100% stacked bar chart to make it clear how passives affect the NPS score as well:

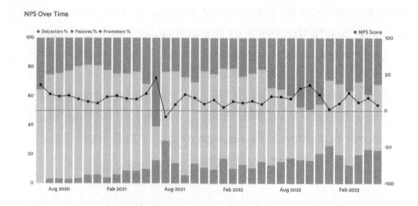

Act on customer feedback

While the score itself gives you a really easy way to know where you stand with your customers at a glance, the true value of NPS comes from the customer feedback. Analyzing and acting on customer feedback insights is what will continue to move your business forward.

Traditional surveys bias customer feedback to what the company wants to hear, not what the customer wants to say. If you're asking the wrong questions, you'll never get the right answers. NPS passes the microphone to the customer, so they can validate or course-correct your business decisions.

> *"I am sooo glad I found you guys. I have been searching for the perfect gift for my 90-year-old grandmother and this is PERFECT! This will mean so much to her. It's like you read my mind!"*

Language is rich with "between the lines" messaging. Emotion and nuance is lost when customers are forced to choose from a selection of pre-defined answers that sterilize feedback. NPS lets the voice of the customer permeate your organization and drive change.

> *"You have some REALLY cool hidden gems, but I have a really hard time finding them. I know they are there, but after a 12-hour workday, I just don't have the patience to go searching."*

When NPS is fully integrated into your organization, it creates a perpetual cycle of product and customer experience improvement. As trends emerge, your teams can address them quickly, and immediately measure the impact they have had, in very human terms.

> *"I was disappointed to find that your packaging was not compostable or biodegradable. What a shame! It's 2021! I can't recommend any service that does not respect the environment."*

Why measure NPS?

NPS is a clear way to align organizations around customer experience. It's easy to understand, and its format is very human. It keeps the focus on the customer.

Regardless of your size or industry, NPS is a great way to understand your customers. Connect with shoppers after their order arrives. Identify why customers choose your software over competitors, Get feedback from guests of your hotel after their stay.

For most companies, feedback arrives via the relatively small percentage of people who contact customer support for specific issues. Everyone has a story, and the vast majority of stories go untold. NPS surfaces feedback from people who you would have not otherwise heard from.

Your detractors are unsatisfied customers who are at risk of leaving you for a competitor. Recurring NPS surveys provide you with the feedback necessary to turn their experience around and monitor customer health to see if your changes are making an impact.

Your happiest customers can also be your brand evangelists. Identify your promoters through NPS surveys and ask them to review you on 3rd-party sites or participate in case studies to keep your reputation strong and promote your brand.

But, there is another side to NPS. The big benefit of NPS: It's simple.

Data is worthwhile ONLY if you do something with it—if it spurs action on your part. If you have a bunch of customer success metrics but don't use them for anything, you're wasting your time.

Simple and useful as it may be, NPS doesn't go without criticism. Some people clearly aren't big fans. Prominent market researchers, usability experts, and academics have all voiced concerns about NPS.

The downsides of simplicity

It's no secret that we like to imagine the world as simpler and more predictable than it actually is. To do that, we construct narratives and frameworks that allow us to make sense of the world.

When you take a short personality test, you get a result that lumps you with all the other ENFPs. When you're born in September, you're a Virgo. If you were good at drawing as a kid, you might have been labeled right-brained.

Problem is, the world is more nuanced than that. Lots of research has refuted Myers-Briggs, right versus left brained, and other lenses you use to view yourself and the world. When you attach a business metric to "one simple question," you're competing with these other simplifications to try to fit a complex network of data into a single number or lens.

Net Promoter Score has been shown to correlate with customer loyalty, retention, and growth—but not always. It does give you an anchor though, a number you can move up and down, a sense of progress.

I am saying, do NOT throw away analytics and your other customer research tools! Don't think that this one simple question will grow your business in your spare time! We know that no single question can tell you everything.

NPS can tell you what your customers think of you, but not necessarily why they feel that way about your brand. This is true of any quantitative metric, of course. And that's why NPS tools should ask the follow up question as I indicated before. I am NOT a fan however, of the question, "What can we do to improve?" From personal experience, we have found that if this is the follow-up question, only 34% of customers will respond with an answer.

The author of the blog, "UserTesting," Jennifer Winter gives this example:

> *Imagine that a company sent out an NPS survey immediately following a customer's purchase. The purchase experience was good, so the customer gave the company a high score.*
>
> *But, a few days later, when the customer received the product, it wasn't what they ordered. The return process was the polar opposite of the checkout process. The customer is now frustrated, upset, and has vowed never to make another purchase. If another*

NPS survey were sent out at this time, chances are this customer would be a vocal detractor.

NPS captures just one point in time with a customer, and the customer's response will depend heavily on their most recent experience. Focusing solely on NPS as a measure of overall CX is a dangerous habit that could eventually turn loyal promoters into detractors.

While many consulting firms that tell you NPS is the be-all-end-all metric, know this: No single survey question can predict your company's success. It is simply used as a metric by which progress in the customer experience initiative can be measured.

Either way, NPS isn't all bad. If anything, it triggers an organization-wide attitude toward improving the customer experience. There's nothing wrong with that. And, if used in conjunction with user research and analytics, NPS can be a solid addition to the conversion research arsenal.

When he lost his Warby Parker glasses on an Acela train heading home to Boston, Michael Parker Mathis learned that great customer service doesn't stop when you leave the office.

Having lost his glasses, Mathis ordered a new pair almost immediately. A few weeks later, Mathis was surprised when he received a package that contained two pairs of glasses and a handwritten note:

Hi Michael, This might be odd...but you sat across from me on the train ride from NYC to Boston a few weeks ago and left your glasses on the train! As luck would have it, I happen to be the GC of Warby Parker, and there is nothing I like more than a good mystery...I hope these find you in good health! (Also, we noticed your lenses were scratched so we made you a fresh pair!)

Sincerely, AK

 Michael John Mathis
July 21

I just experienced possibly the very best customer service of all time. A few weeks ago, I accidentally left my beloved Warby Parker reading glasses on the Acela. Annoyed, I bought myself another, identical, pair the following day. Today I received an unexpected package containing not one, but two pair of those same reading glasses, a copy of "On The Road" by Jack Kerouac and the following note: "Hi Michael, This might be odd... but you sat across from me on the train ride from NYC to Boston a few weeks ago and left your glasses on the train! As luck would have it, I happen to be the GC of Warby Parker, and there is nothing I like more than a good mystery... I hope these find you in good health! (also, we noticed your lenses were scratched so we made you a fresh pair!) Sincerely, AK

I am so impressed! What a remarkable person and company. They have a customer for life!

Mathis was so impressed that he posted about the experience on Facebook, "They have a customer for life!"

Stories like Mathis' lost Warby Parker glasses are uncommon, but so are the outsized reactions, which is what makes going above and beyond worthwhile.

Employee Engagement Surveys

According to SHRM (Society of Human Resource Management), *"employee engagement surveys measure employees' commitment, motivation, sense of purpose and passion for their work and organization."*

A carefully designed and conducted employee survey can reveal a great deal of information about employee perceptions that management can use to improve the workplace. Organization responsiveness to employee feedback leads to higher retention rates, lower absenteeism, improved productivity, better customer experience, and higher employee morale. The simple fact that the organization is conducting a survey can send a positive message to employees that their opinions are valued. In addition, managers can gain insights into issues affecting their departments or business units that allow them to manage more effectively. Conversely, if the senior management team is not fully committed and ready to really listen to and, most importantly, act on what employees are saying, then conducting a survey can falsely raise expectations among employees, leading to an employee relations disaster.

Organizations should conduct surveys of employees on a regular basis—most companies elect to ask their employees for feedback annually. Requesting regular feedback shows employees that the company actually cares about how they perceive their work environment. Choosing when to conduct the survey should take several things into consideration. Avoiding peak holiday seasons is usually best to ensure a maximum response from employees. Scheduling the survey during the organization's historically slow periods is also advisable so that employees will have the necessary time to devote to the survey. Finally, it might be good to avoid conducting the survey during cycles that could skew the results either positivity or negatively. Bonus season or high-stress periods can provide an unrealistic picture of normal employee satisfaction if year-over-year normal operating results are the objective.

However, when an organization is in the midst of a major corporate change (e.g., massive layoffs or a significant merger or restructuring or a pandemic), conducting a survey might not be advised because employees tend to be somewhat reserved and fearful during such times. To generate honest feedback, an atmosphere of trust must be present. If not, the survey might actually end up doing more harm than good.

SURVEY DESIGN

A survey can't measure or fix every problem at once, and you will lose time and money if you try to approach it this way. To create an engagement survey that gives you valuable data, you must be strategic about how to generate an actionable outcome. Focus on pinpointing a specific problem (the *what*), identifying drivers that contribute to the problem (the *why*), and then begin tailoring your questions (the *how*).

1. The *What*: Determine your focus area

Identifying one focus area helps provide a clear goal for the employee engagement survey and outlines what you want to achieve. This is an exercise in determining the *scope* of your inquiry and *what* you are asking employees about.

The first thing to do is brainstorm and make a list of problems that you think may be affecting employee engagement. You'll want to do the following:

- **Consult company leadership**. Ideally, leaders have a finger on the pulse of the company, understanding the organizational culture and strategic objectives. Include managers and leaders from different departments, particularly HR.

- **Review past surveys**. Has your company executed employee engagement surveys in the past? What problems were identified? Did you address or improve employee engagement problems, or are they still an issue? If problems on previous surveys are still an issue and have not been addressed, a new survey may not be received with a willingness to complete it, honestly and sincerely. Problems can vary from survey to survey, so make sure that you identify current issues and action areas.

- **Use exit surveys**. While exit surveys are not an unbiased look at a company, they can provide some relatively honest feedback from former employees. If you have had employees leave recently, it can be worth seeing whether there are any common problems they identify in their exit surveys.

Now it's time to narrow your scope. You need to pick one area of focus that will ultimately help define the desired outcome of the survey. This process starts by determining possible focus areas from your brainstorm and prioritizing which one(s) to tackle. Start by asking these questions for each possible area:

1. Is this a problem that we can solve within a reasonable time frame?

2. How often is the problem occurring?

3. How costly or problematic is the issue?

4. Does the company have the resources to solve the problem?

5. What is the main benefit of solving the problem?

After going through this prioritization process with the other problems, choose the one that is both most immediate and solvable.

2. The *Why*: Determine your drivers

Now that your focus area is determined, you need to identify the drivers of the problem—the areas within the work environment that are the biggest factors of the problem and thus lower your employees' levels of engagement.

To decide what these drivers are, try using the "5 Whys Analysis" to break down the drivers of the problem:

- Write down the problem.

- Ask "Why is this problem occurring?"

- Determine a reason the problem exists.

- Ask "Why is this occurring?" and document. Do this for each reason.

- Keep asking "Why?" until you reach the root cause.

For example, your company decides that its biggest problem is that employees in the customer service department are reporting that they feel burned out. You can start by asking the first why:

- *Why*? The workload is too much for employees to realistically handle.

- *Why*? Management expects employees to close too many tickets each day.

- *Why*? We have gained 50 new clients over the past year.

- *Why*? Our sales team has gained four new employees.

This gets you to the root of the problem—you are adding clients faster than customer service employees. Summarize and clarify as you go to ensure that each possible reason is understood. You may need to ask "why" more or less than five times (as seen above) to find the true cause. There also may be more than one possible reason for the problem.

This analysis will give you a *hypothesis* about possible problems that employees are experiencing—not a surefire answer. They are the building blocks of your engagement survey and should be used to shape the content in the engagement survey, not taken as gospel when determining why employees are feeling disengaged.

3. The *How*: Build your engagement survey

You now have the foundation to design a customized survey. Continuing with the previous example, let's take a look at how to tackle the problem of burnout:

1. **Problem**: Employees in your customer service department are feeling burned out.

2. **Drivers**: Employee workload, manager expectations, training.

3. **Potential roots**: Increase in clients not supported by hiring, management.

Based on this information, you can begin crafting individual questions for the survey. Keep it short and focused by asking tailored questions that are necessary to analyze the data, but don't ask questions that put words in your employees' mouths.

For example, "***Do you think we hired too many new salespeople and not enough customer service reps* [yes/no]**" restricts an employee's ability to really give feedback. It only reflects one narrow perspective. Instead, try a set of statements like these:

- My manager sets clear goals for my performance. [Strongly disagree – Strongly agree]

- I frequently struggle to meet my expected quota of service tickets. [Strongly disagree – Strongly agree]

- I am confident in my ability to tackle day-to-day challenges at my job. [Strongly disagree – Strongly agree]

- If I could change one thing about my job/department, it would be [open answer].

This series of statements investigates whether management, training or an increase in clients is more likely the cause of stress *and* allows employees to speak in their own words about what they see as the biggest engagement problem.

Rather than a simple yes/no, this gets at the potential drivers of your problem. If employees rate their managers and their confidence about tackling challenges poorly, better management support is needed. If they simply struggle to meet a quota and express a desire to add a team member, it's likely an increase in customers.

Write as many questions or statements as you need to ask about all of your drivers. The number will depend on your topics and your audience, but if you find yourself covering too much ground, it's OK to limit the survey to fewer problems.

Now What?

Congratulations! You have completed your employee engagement survey and now what?

First, use the percentage of responses as your initial matrix for measurement. If, on your first survey, 78% of employees responded but, a year later, only 62% respond, ask yourself what that is telling you.

When responding to results, it's tempting to immediately dive into making changes—after all, you didn't run the survey just for fun, and you want employees to know that you hear them and value their input. However, if you jump into making changes without deeply understanding what the results of your employee engagement survey are telling you, you risk creating as many new problems as you fix.

It's important to approach this with the same thoughtful mindset you'd use when developing your company's next quarterly financial plan. By following the eight steps below, you can ensure that you get the most value out of your survey results, and that the changes you implement based on those results address the issues your employees have brought to your attention.

1. Review Results

When employee engagement survey results become available, the first step is to share them with your executive team. When you sort results and drill down into team data and experience by demographic, executives can learn things like which groups are having an inconsistent experience with impartiality and equity. When you take this more granular look at data, executives get a clearer picture of what employees are telling them.

2. Reflect

Leaders must take time to review and internalize feedback before they jump into action. Feedback provides essential insight into a company's leadership and the experience of employees. It can be hard to hear, but it can also be the most valuable tool for improvement if leaders learn from it. Encourage leaders to take time to absorb and process employee feedback before going any further.

3. Align & Set Intentions

Once leaders have had time for reflection, the executive team should meet again to discuss the data and how they plan to proceed. Ideally, executives communicated with employees about the survey before sending it out, so employees understand the purpose and expected outcomes of the process.

It's easier to maximize the full value of the employee engagement survey results when executives share a clear understanding of what their ideal company culture is and where the gaps are.

Consider the following factors:

- Does everyone in the organization have a clear picture of your desired culture? Can employees connect that picture to the company's values and how the values help achieve this culture?

- Do employees understand how your desired culture helps the company accomplish its mission?

- Do leaders understand what expectations your desired culture creates for them and their leadership style? Do people processes reward desired leadership behavior while also holding leaders accountable?

- Do leaders understand the connection between survey results and employees' perceptions and expectations of leadership?

4. Provide Transparent Communication

Your organization's initial reaction to the survey sets the tone for how you go about taking action. Many of the lists of the 'best companies to work for' roll out survey-driven changes using a cascaded approach. This process often begins with an organization-wide communication from the CEO that might share high-level results, thank employees for their participation, and commit to taking action.

Next, leaders at all levels take the opportunity to discuss results transparently with their teams, ideally in a way that shares more relevant details about organizational and departmental level results and allows for an open dialogue to begin.

5. Conduct a listening tour

Leaders at all levels can conduct listening tours with employees in order to gain more specific insight to make meaningful improvement throughout the organization. Whether leaders choose to do this with informal brown-bag lunches or more formal meetings, documenting the meetings and letting employees know how leaders will be following up ensures they understand what comes next and shows them how important this process is to you.

6. Target Areas for Improvement & Establish Specific Plans

It's often best to target one or two areas of focus to make lasting improvements. Often, one area is identified as an organization-wide focus with the second area specifically relating to department/leader level results. The best strategies focus on how management is leading.

For example, survey results that reflect improvement opportunities in communication may indicate a need for meaningful dialogue (asking questions, being present, eye contact) rather than a need for more meetings and emails.

Common Practices for Leaders:

- Target one or two areas of improvement and ensure areas are actionable

- Get employee input and feedback by asking questions like:

    ♦ *Which areas would make the greatest positive impact to their experience?*

    ♦ *What does "great" look like in this area?* Have them share an example of when it was happening at its best.

- Document and communicate plans or commitment for improvement (be specific and include measures of success)

- Engage a peer, a coach, or leader as an accountability partner that leaders regularly connect with for advice and support

7. Execute

Now, it's time for your patient, methodical approach to employee engagement surveys to pay off. Roll out your people practices and programs.

You've taken a data-driven approach and infused it with employee input throughout the process. Feels good, doesn't it?

8. Evaluate Progress

To demonstrate your commitment to taking meaningful action, and to make sure that your changes are having desired effects, continue to communicate with your employees.

A few ways to do this:

- Pulse surveys to measure progress on areas of focus

- Follow up listening sessions to gauge progress and seek more feedback

- Department meetings to discuss progress and get feedback by asking questions such as:

  - *Are you experiencing improvement in this area?*

  - *What is working? What are examples of where this is happening well?*

  - *What additional ideas for improvement would you recommend?*

Engaged employees are the foundation of successful companies. If employees aren't engaged with their work, then they're less likely to make the impact that their managers hope for and even more less likely to influence the customer experience. When employees are engaged, they're brand ambassadors, customer satisfaction gurus, and they even take fewer sick days. Engaged employees are the backbone of successful businesses.

In their book, 'Contented Cows STILL Give Better Milk', authors Bill Catlette and Richard Hadden state, "The truth is that most of our products and service, technologies, methods, tools, and strategies can all be copied. However, it's not as easy to duplicate a focused, caring workforce."

Amazon Prime, the company's two-day shipping service, has converted one-time shoppers into Amazon addicts who buy almost everything from the e-retailer.

Amazon has software engineer Charlie Ward to thank for that. Ward suggested the idea of a free shipping service through a suggestion box feature on Amazon's internal website. Another employee came up with the "Prime" name and other Amazon executives, including CEO Jeff Bezos, hatched the idea of the free two-day shipping offer.

A challenge the team came across was selecting an annual fee for the free shipping service. No one knew how many customers would join or if Prime would make a difference in their purchasing habits. The team ultimately chose $79 mostly because it's a prime number.

"It was never about the 79 dollars. It was mainly about changing people's mentality so they wouldn't shop anywhere else," said Vijay Ravindran, who worked on the Prime team and is now the chief digital officer for The Washington Post.

Regardless of how the team came up with a $79 fee, it worked.

The team that worked on the service predicted that Amazon Prime would break even in two years. Instead, it broke even within three months of launching.

After customers became Prime members, they spent as much as 150% more at Amazon. Subscription members ordered more often and, after paying the (then) $79 fee, they started buying things at Amazon that they probably wouldn't have in the past.

Amazon Prime worked because Bezos was "immediately enchanted by the idea" and latched onto it.

Bezos took a wild guess when he priced Prime at $79 but he trusted his team and instincts. Ward's idea went from a simple suggestion to an incredibly successful Amazon service that changes the buying habits of customers.

The process of launching Amazon Prime brings up an important point for management: have an employee suggestion program in place to listen to your employees and act on their ideas. You won't know if an idea will prove to be an incredible success until you give it a chance.

Total Sales Growth

More than half of private employers now share how their organizations are faring financially with employees.

- Although they are not obligated to do so, private companies can benefit from sharing financial information with their employees.

- Employees feel more engaged and empowered when they have access to company financial data.

- Companies should explain the information and offer context, so it is not overwhelming to employees.

A growing number of employers are no longer leaving their staff in the dark on the company's financial performance, new research finds. A study from Robert Half Management Resources revealed that 56% of private organizations provide at least some employees with regular updates on the company's financial performance, up from 32% in 2014.

The research shows that one-quarter of employers share fiscal information with all their workers.

"Though not a requirement for private companies, providing insights on financial performance instills in employees a sense of ownership, which often leads to improved employee engagement and productivity," Tim Hird, executive director of Robert Half Management Resources, said.

So-called "open-book management" offers several benefits. The main benefits are:

1. **Accountability**. By sharing the results, you are holding both the leadership and the employees accountable for the results of their efforts.

2. **Increased sales**. Studies show boosts of 1–2% in companies that open their books to employees.

3. **Enhanced understanding**. By sharing information, you help your employees understand how the company operates, and they become better workers and, potentially, internal entrepreneurs.

4. **Empowers employees**. Employees will be on the lookout for ways they can improve operations.

5. **Gives the sense of being a stakeholder**. Employees who are trusted with vital financial information feel that they are part of the team.

6. **Increased job satisfaction and better performance**. Employees who feel trusted and valued are more loyal and more engaged and feel a part of the end-to-end customer experience.

One of our clients, a plastics manufacturer recently told me, when referring about 'numbers transparency' as I like to call it, "*I don't have just employees anymore. I have entrepreneurs who are looking to find ways to make more money for the firm.*"

Most of the employers surveyed believe employees want to learn more about how their company is faring financially.

"Professionals want to work for organizations that are open with staff about the health of the business," Hird said. *"Discuss opportunities and challenges facing the organization as it grows, and invite ideas to help the firm meet its goals."*

To help employers who want to be more upfront about their financial status, here are several tips:

1. **Decide what to share**. You not only have to determine what details you are comfortable sharing, but you also want to know what employees want to hear about. If you are unsure about what and how much info to provide, consider reaching out to peers and consultants to learn what insights other companies are giving their employees.

2. **Create a schedule**. If you are going to give financial updates, you should do so on a regular basis. Let employees know how often they should expect financial updates. It is important to stick to your schedule, even when you have to share bad news.

3. **Show them their impact**. When discussing financial performance, connect the dots for employees by showing them how their work is contributing to the company's bottom line. By doing so, you will give them more incentive to better align their work and ideas to the organization's goals.

4. **Explain the numbers**. It's one thing to dump a bunch of financial details on your workers, but it's another to actually explain what they mean. In addition to a formal presentation on the fiscal data, have bosses be prepared to answer any follow-up questions their staff may have.

5. **Add some context**. Some small business owners are hesitant to share details with workers who may not be familiar with the data, out of concern that it may cause anxiety instead of providing comfort. Once employees have grasped one financial concept, introduce additional or more complex data.

6. **Omit salary data**. It may be a distraction to include details on compensation, and you could end up causing dissension and drama, especially if individual information is discernible.

7. **Keep it simple**. Some employees may be entirely unfamiliar with financial jargon, but that doesn't mean they don't want the information. Spell it out, and gradually increase the sophistication of the information as their knowledge base grows.

The Sales Growth metric tracks the bottom line of a company and looks to see if the number of sales has increased over a certain time period or since a customer experience initiative began. Companies that focus on customer experience tend to make more sales, so this number should ideally increase with more emphasis placed on the customer experience. It is, however, fairly elusive as a definitive measurement because there are so many factors that can affect sales numbers. It is just a great KPI that everyone can be a cheerleader for.

Customer Retention

The percentage of customers who remain with a company over a period of time.

Retention Rate (%) = (# of Customers at End of Period - # of Customers Acquired During Period) / Total # of Customers at Start of Period

Similar to customer churn rate, customer retention is extremely valuable for company growth. In fact, a 5% increase in customer retention can increase company revenue by 25–95% (Bain & Company). It is still very important to drive growth through acquiring new customers, but the cost savings of building long-standing customer relationships are significant in comparison to the effort spent on acquiring new ones. This is why customer retention is a great measurement of customer experience.

Neglecting existing customers in pursuit of new ones is a common mistake. While customer acquisition *is* important for business growth, meeting the needs of your existing customer base can be just as critical. Businesses who implement a strong customer retention strategy will reap the benefits.

Repeat customers are more profitable

Compared to new customers, repeat customers tend to spend more and are more likely to try your new products/services. Businesses should therefore work toward building a customer base with trust and loyalty toward their brand, to see their profits increase over time. Check out these statistics:

1. 61% of small businesses report that more than half of their revenue comes from repeat customers. [Blakesly]

2. On average, loyal customers are worth up to ten times as much as their first purchase. [Marketing Tech Blog]

3. It can cost five times more to acquire new customers than it does to keep current ones. [The National Law Review]

4. A 5% increase in customer retention can increase a company's profitability by 75%. [Bain & Company]

5. Reducing your customer defection rate by 5% can increase your profitability by 25 to 125%. [DestinationCRM]

6. 82% of companies agree that retention is cheaper to execute than acquisition. [Econsultancy]

7. The average repeat customer spends 67% more in their 31st–36th months of their relationship with a business than in months 0–6. [Bain & Company]

8. 89% of customers begin business with a competitor following a poor customer experience. [Oracle]

9. It takes twelve positive customer experiences to make up for one negative experience. (Parature)

10. A 2% increase in retention has the same effect as decreasing costs by 10%. [*Leading on the Edge of Chaos*]

As you can see above, the impact of customer retention can be felt from your bottom line to your marketing tactics (e.g., SEO), cost of sales, and customer service. It is a metric, behind which, all of your people can measure and support.

You can save on marketing

Your existing customers already *know* about your products and services—so why not gear efforts toward retaining them, rather than focusing solely on marketing to potential new customers?

Afterall, word-of-mouth recommendations by loyal customers can be more lucrative and credible than any marketing—according to Yotpo, 60% of loyal customers will talk about their favorite brands with people in their social circle.

Customer retention can drive customer acquisition

Attracting new customers requires continuously honing your products and services to stay one step ahead of your competitors, and loyal customers can help you achieve this by providing valuable feedback.

Talk to your existing customers—ask them what they like and dislike about your products and services, and what sort of changes could help to improve their experience with you. Acting on this invaluable feedback to meet your customers' needs and improve your product and service is how you truly set yourself apart from your competitors and spot new opportunities for growth.

Retaining your customers using insight

So, how do you retain your ever-important existing customers? A strong customer retention strategy will involve learning more about your customers' expectations and experiences with you. Using a deep insight into customer experience to guide your product and service, you can ensure you are keeping pace with customers' ever-changing needs and are giving them no reason to look elsewhere. Show that you value them, and they will value you right back.

Understand your customer's persona

Understanding buyer personas is a crucial component of customer retention, particularly for the sales and marketing departments. After all, the marketing team needs to know to whom they are marketing, and the sales team needs to know to whom they are selling. I stole this from my days in the marketing profession and I think it is a fun way to get your people engaged in thinking about persona and customer experience.

But once you sit down to craft your customer personas, you may find yourself staring blankly at a white screen for some time, wondering where on earth you're supposed to begin. Before you spend time and money on research, ask yourself the questions below to help you develop your personas.

Customer Persona Questions to Ask When Identifying Your Audience

1. Questions About Their Personal Background

Describe your personal demographics.

Describe your educational background.

Describe your career path.

Questions About Their Company

In which industry or industries does your company work?

What is the size of your company (revenue, employees)?

Questions About Their Role

What is your job role? Your title?

Whom do you report to? Who reports to you?

What does a typical day look like?

Which skills are required to do your job?

What knowledge and which tools do you use in your job?

Questions About Their Challenges

What are your biggest challenges?

What are you responsible for?

What does it mean to be successful in your role?

Questions About How They Learn

How do you learn about new information for your job?

Which publications or blogs do you read?

Which associations and social networks do you participate in?

Questions About Their Shopping Preferences

How do you prefer to interact with vendors?

Do you use the internet to research vendors or products? If yes, how do you search for information?

Describe a recent purchase.

Once you've gone through this exercise and worked out any lingering questions about what makes your persona tick, browse through some stock imagery and find an actual picture to associate with your persona. Going through this exercise forces you to clarify an image of your target audience in your entire organization's mind that will help keep your messaging consistent. Make it fun by having a contest for your employees to come up with the image! Then NAME the persona and put his/her photo around the office to remind people who they serve.

Another useful exercise is to practice being able to identify your buyer persona so you can tailor your communications. How will you know when you're talking to this persona? Is it their job title? Something about the way they talk or carry a conversation? Their pain points? How they found your company? Once you've established not only who your persona is, but also how you can identify them when you encounter one or another, your employees will be able to maintain a consistent voice that is still customized to each person they talk to.

So, let's take a look at a couple of companies who are incredibly successful in understanding their customers' persona…

Seventeen

Let's start with a little bit of history, shall we? An article on The Awl about the history of *Seventeen* magazine highlighted the magazine's target persona back in 1950. They created a persona named Teena based on survey data from teenage girls and their mothers during the mid 1940s. Here's how they described Teena in the article:

Teena the High School Girl has a peck of problems. She's what older folks call an awkward adolescent -- too tall, too plump, too shy -- a little too much of a lot of little things. But they're big things to Teena. And though she doesn't always take her troubles to her mother, Teena writes her favorite magazine for the tip-off on the clothes she wears, the food she eats, the lipstick she wields, the room she bunks in, the budget she keeps, the boy she has a crush on.

Now, **Seventeen** has gone through many adaptations of who their prime buyer persona is—this is just who they were targeting in the 1950s. But just look how it manifested itself in their magazine:

As you would see from their covers if you were looking, there was a strong focus in their feature content on Teena's insecurities and hang-ups—not that I endorse capitalizing on young girls' insecurities; this is simply a demonstration, for better or worse, of personas aligning well with a brand's marketing. For instance, they had content like "Diet with Ice Cream," an entire "Boy-Girl Issue," and a story called "Dates (how to get)." These are all things that high school girls are insecure about, and Seventeen channeled what was going on in high school girls' minds to power their content strategy.

Zipcar

Zipcar's main buyer persona is the millennial urban dweller. Zipcar's services are typically offered in large cities around the world, with high populations of millennials who either can't afford a car, or don't see the need to own one in the city. With its sharing-focused business model, users pay hourly or daily rates for use of a communal car, without having to worry about paying for things like gas and insurance. What a nice, unburdened lifestyle!

When you look at the channels and tone that Zipcar uses in its marketing, it is obvious that this free-wheelin' (pun intended) audience is who they're targeting. Just look at this tweet aimed at the millennial world traveler, for instance:

Zipcar
@Zipcar

Did you know your Zipcard works in
Barcelona too? Realmente! buzz.mw/-N7z_y
cc @AvanCarSharing #getoutandzip
twitpic.com/b5bsqw

← Reply ⭤ Retweet ★ Favorite

By Zipcar @Zipcar

Or this tweet with the whimsical, and again, free wheelin'
hashtag, #thatswhereiroll:

 **Zipcar**
@Zipcar

Following

@shanecbingham + @MeganSense_,
@ZipcarVancouver is lucky to have you in
town. Email twitter@zipcar.com to get your
#thatswhereiroll prize.

← Reply ⭤ Retweet ★ Favorite

Although customer persona is primarily used as a marketing tool, I take clients through this exercise because I think it is vital to understanding your customer better than anyone else—and working with them in a way in which they WANT to be worked with, NOT the way you have necessarily worked with them in the past.

Employee Retention

It might not be the most glamorous of CX strategies, but effective management of employee turnover can make or break a company's customer experience. One of the most effective tactics for improving the customer experience (CX) is also among the least glamorous. For all of the management attention focused on "shiny object" CX strategies (such as digital transformation, artificial intelligence, predictive analytics, etc.), it's the simple influence of *employee turnover* that can make or break a company's customer experience.

I was reminded of this in a recent client engagement where we looked at the correlation between the company's employee turnover rate and its Net Promoter Score. As the graphic below illustrates, we found a rather striking relationship between these two measures (something we've observed at other firms, as well):

Relationship Between NPS & Turnover Rate

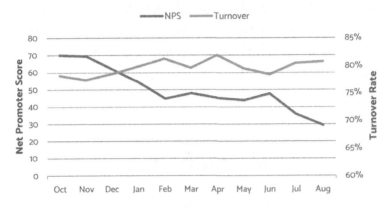

For this particular company, the NPS and turnover trends were like mirror images of one another. When turnover fell, NPS rose. When turnover rose, NPS fell. (For the statisticians out there, in this example, the two measures had a strong negative correlation of 0.74.) What accounts for this connection between employee turnover and customer experience? It boils down to three factors:

- **Focus**. In a high turnover environment, a business' focus necessarily shifts from development to survival. Management doesn't have the luxury to concentrate on things like customer experience, because they're consumed with the Herculean task of filling staffing gaps as quickly as they're created.

- **Fitness**. By definition, a high turnover workforce is a less experienced workforce. Newly hired employees may be good people, but they will lack the expertise and competence of more seasoned staff. As a result, the workforce's overall fitness to effectively serve customers is compromised.

- **Familiarity**. In many types of businesses, customers like working with familiar faces—the retail clothing store associate who knows my style, the insurance agent who knows my coverage needs, the auto mechanic who knows my car. In these relationship businesses, high turnover is jarring to the customer because they crave consistency, but are forced to deal with new employees time and time again.

To put the impact of turnover in perspective, consider the retail industry, where (according to the National Retail Federation) the average employee turnover rate is a little over 60 percent. That means if you're a store manager, *every year you're replacing almost two-thirds of your staff*. Think about the effect that has on how quickly and competently employees are able to serve customers. It's a huge issue made bigger by the fact that many companies don't have very good training programs for new staff.

It comes as little surprise, then, that organizations known for excelling in customer experience also tend to exhibit below average employee turnover (Costco, Publix, Wegmans, USAA, and Southwest Airlines among them).

The minimization of employee turnover may not be the most glamorous and exciting of customer experience strategies, *but it is a critical one*. When business leaders neglect to manage turnover effectively and address its root causes, it inevitably sows the seeds for future customer experience failure.

The key is to hire the right people, to be deliberate in onboarding and training them, and to equip them with the tools and knowledge needed for success. Such a focus on the employee experience helps improve engagement and reduce turnover. And that's critical to any company's success, because if your employees keep heading for the exits, your customers will soon follow.

Since the topic of Employee Experience grew out of employee engagement, companies are not always clear about the return on investment. Well it's now very clear that when employee satisfaction is high, customer satisfaction and financial growth follow. As I often tell clients in our conversations, your employees "are" your company, so the more productive and engaged they are, the faster your company will grow.

CRITICAL QUESTION #9

How Do We to Respond to Negative
Feedback?

NEGATIVE FEEDBACK, LIKE a complaint, is good for you. It helps your company improve and grow better than the competition. However, if a disgruntled customer takes it to the web, everybody on Facebook, Google My Business, or Yelp can see the one-star rating and their poor experience with your organization.

That doesn't have to ruin your branding on the web. A bad review can become a good opportunity to show you care about your customer.

Here are seven proven steps to respond to negative feedback and turn an uncomfortable situation into something constructive for customers and your business.

Step #1. Address the customer by name

It's just a little psychological trick, and you may think that there's no need to do this. Sure, you can start your response with a quick hello, or a "Dear Sir," but it's not as potent as writing the person's name.

Unless you're running anonymized surveys, the name of the person is stated in the review, so it wouldn't take a lot of effort to find it out. By saying their name and referring to their feedback, you show that it's not an automatic scripted response, and they're talking to someone who's going to take care of their problem. If the issue they have with your business can be solved at all, the reviewer can be more cooperative if you start the conversation in a friendly way. This restaurant owner did it the wrong way.

1/6/2019 · It actually incredibly clean if you're willing to take a mini tour inside of our restaurant. Btw those garbage cans belong to the tenants upstairs. The left over from someone was placed on top of their cans and fell off while we were operating our business, I had my staff cleaned it up right when I spotted the mess. Kung Food is going for its 5th year, and we ain't going anywhere for the next 5. Thanks for the unbiased reviews. Yee Bayarea representa ya feel me, if you're from da Yay then show some love and respect for the small business here. If you're ain't from around, then I won't blame you for being the flaw picking nagging dude at all. Peace and love y'all Read less

Source: Kung Food/Yelp

Step #2. Apologize to the customer

You may be thinking that this customer knows nothing about the business and isn't justified for putting up a review. You may think they were in a bad mood and you couldn't do much in terms of service. You may think it's a competitor, not a genuine reviewer.

Either way, you have to apologize to them to get their attention. Take a look at how this restaurant owner handled a one-star review on Yelp. He disagrees with the reviewer but apologizes nonetheless.

10/19/2018 · Hi

Sorry to hear that we could not make you happy.

I am the owner and I have enough experience in this industry. I also take a lot of good reviews about my service and I would love to hear more detailed feedback from you about our service. Your review is pretty simple and does not really explain what was missing with your service and it looks like you have a lot of knowledge about this industry. Could you please explain what was exactly wrong with your table?

I would be happy to give you full refund since we couldn't make you happy.

Looking forward to hearing from you.

Best Regards,

Read less

Source: Lokma/Yelp

Step #3. Sympathize with the customer's problem

Just as in the previous step, you don't have to agree with the customer to understand their frustration. Imagine yourself in their shoes. You come expecting a great experience, but it's far below your expectations. It can potentially ruin your day.

This is why a person who left a negative review deserves your sympathy. Make sure you tell them you understand their feelings too, and be somewhat vulnerable. Here's how this hotel manager does this.

Responded Apr 23, 2019

Dear ▓▓▓▓▓▓

I am very sorry for encountering this issue. This is by no means acceptable and wish to better understand your stay with us. If time permits, please contact me at Ulices▓▓▓▓▓▓▓▓▓▓▓▓▓

This is not the accepted or normal, but Hotel Staff is empowered to quickly act and make the situation right. I can understand your frustration with the stay described and if given the opportunity to know more about your visit then we can move forward. Guest comments are very powerful to understanding the direction which direction we are headed and in doing so we take every comment to the utmost seriousness.

I hope we can have the privilege to speak and we thank your honesty.

Source: Millenium Biltmore/Tripadvisor

If the experience at your business ruined someone's day, they may be writing the review in anger. Words of sympathy are the least an angry person expects. When they hear them, they may be more willing to understand you as well. They are looking for what you are going to do about it, either for them or for your customers in the future.

Step #4. State that you're solving the problem

In some cases, a reviewer who doesn't like your company is only guided by preferences. In many others, there was a problem with your business. Your service person was rude, shipment took longer than expected, or the product arrived damaged. Basically, the customer created a review instead of talking to support. If that's the case, you have to help the reviewer. But taking the matter to your customer support team doesn't cut it. The review is on display now, and you have to put your reaction on display as well.

★ ★ ☆ ☆ ☆ 6 months ago
I've been in here twice now and the edible section is good. The pre-rolled however...The first time I came in I got the newbie deal of 2 good sized mixed joints for $1. I returned and paid $16 for the Blue Dream preroll. Opened it at home ...
More

 Like   ＜ Share

Response from the owner 4 months ago
Hey⬛⬛⬛, sorry this is coming a bit late. I have a feeling you may have gotten one of our "shorty" joints by accident as all of our $16 joints are at least a gram of bud. Swing by some time and we will make it up to you!

Source: Searchdispensary

From the perspective of a prospective customer, seeing you respond to a random review offering help is a good sign. A potential customer learns you care about your users and can sort things out if something goes wrong. Mention reaching out to the reviewer to solve the problem, and the impact of a negative review will be minimized.

Step #5. Offer a gift

Another way to try to give a reviewer a more positive impression of your business is by asking them for a second chance. If the problem they've had is out of the ordinary, get the client to come back by offering a gift.

It can be a discount, or free shipping, depending on your type of business. However, the problem they complained about can be a regular one. If this is the case, asking them to come back before you fix it is just counterproductive.

Step #6. Ask the customer to change the review

Did you fix the problem the reviewer had? Did they come back for a discount and loved your business? It's time to ask them to change the review. Don't ask about it publicly, and don't be too pushy. If the person liked your business after they gave it a second chance, they will be willing to do it themselves. If they don't change it, after all, it's okay. You've done the bulk of review-related PR already.

Step #7. Put up with negative reviews

Some reviewers just don't like your organization. It's the price, the style, or one negative experience they've had with you. This customer took it out on a restaurant even though she liked the food.

Source: LaLe/Yelp

You can't do anything to change their opinion. The good thing is you don't have to. Respond with grace, apologize, and focus on getting more positive reviews instead of changing negative ones.

How to Gather Positive & Negative Customer Feedback

It can be daunting to scan social media to find feedback about your business. Getting feedback on your own social media page or on specialized websites is easier to monitor, but it's still on the reactive, not proactive side. Monitor your performance by gathering feedback yourself. This will make sure any negative online reviews never appear in the first place.

Gathering feedback from your clients is easier than you may imagine. It can boil down to showing a non-verbal CSAT survey at the bottom of a webpage or at your cash register. If you can get instant feedback and offer an explanation, you can prevent the customer from ever posting it in the first place.

When I was employed as an assistant practice administrator of a large ophthalmology practice in Northern Illinois, we had an internal motto of "replace + 1." That meant anytime we encountered a patient with a legitimate complaint about something, we were empowered to not only make it better but to add something to really take it to the next level (a 'plus one').

One day we had a patient who was placed in an exam room which was the farthest away from the front. It was down a small hallway toward our back door, so no one walks past that room on their way up and down the hallway. Our process when placing a patient in an exam room was to turn on a small colored light on a panel outside of the door that indicated that a patient was ready for a certain doctor in a certain room. It is a great system when the humans do their job correctly! Unfortunately, the technician forgot to turn on the light and no one knew the patient was waiting. She stayed there for TWO HOURS and never came out to ask why she was being overlooked.

There was another rule in our office: "*She/He who first encounters the angry patient owns them to the completion of their problem.*" Meaning, you find it, you fix it.

At 4 p.m. I was headed out the back door for an early weekend and I walked right past this room. When I glanced in and saw the patient just sitting there in an angry pose, I knew I had just inherited a problem. After inquiring about the situation, I found out she had been waiting all this time and, to make matters worse, she had opera tickets in downtown Chicago that night and because of our mistake it was already too late for her to make opening curtain.

Solution: I gave her the option to leave immediately with a return appointment and a promise that I would personally expedite her through the system, OR I could go get the doctor right that minute and have him come immediately to her room. She chose to wait since leaving in a hurry would not solve her ruined plans for the evening.

While the doctor was taking care of her, I checked with the administrator, and we agreed to replace her opera tickets at our expense. Using this *replace + one* philosophy we were able to turn an extremely angry patient into a gracious one who understood that human mistakes happen.

Laurie Guest, CSP

Keynote Speaker and Trainer

CRITICAL QUESTION #10

Where Do We Get Started?

Listening Tour

I **BELIEVE THAT** this all begins with the 'voice of the employee.' We developed the listening tour as a type of focus group of front-line employees, middle managers, and C-Suite executives. I would suggest that you bring a non-partial, third party in for a day (to assure anonymity) to ask vital questions of these three groups.

Each session should be scheduled for about ninety minutes and there should be very specific questions asked of each group. The following will get you started with your front-line employees but make sure you customize more questions to get the responses to questions that are of concern to you right now.

1. On a scale of 1-10, ten being 'absolutely' and one being 'absolutely not,' would you recommend (name of your organization) to your friends and family if the need arose?

2. On a scale of 1-10, ten being 'absolutely' and one being 'absolutely not,' would you recommend (name of your organization) as a place for your friends and family to work?

3. Does (name of your organization) recognize employees?

4. Does (name of your organization) recognize employees often enough?

5. What type of recognition would you recommend moving forward?

6. Does the organization have a values statement? If so, can you tell me what it says?

7. Does the organization have a service standards policy? If so, can you tell me what it says?

8. Does the organization have a service recovery policy? If so, can you describe it to me?

9. Does the C-Suite do an adequate job of welcoming new employees?

10. Does the C-Suite do an adequate job of 'rounding' (a term stolen from healthcare which means to visit different departments and make themselves available for feedback, questions, and concerns)?

11. Does middle management do an adequate job of 'rounding'?

12. Does your CEO conduct any type of all-employee forum? If so, what is your opinion and how could they be made better?

13. Is your CEO available to you when you have a suggestion, question, or concern?

14. What can we do to make our customer experience better?

15. Does your manager/supervisor hold some type of weekly 'huddle'? (Short, standing meeting to address what's working and what's not working?)

CX Council

Immediately establish a Customer Experience Council. This is the team responsible for providing on-going leadership to improving customer experience. They will be the 'hub" of information for both the Service Advisors and the Organizational Project Teams and will also guide to ensure the CX initiative takes place effectively. They meet every two weeks and the team is made up of 60% management and 40% front-line workers.

Then, assign one 'project coach' from the CX Council to oversee a specific Organizational Project Team.

CX Advisors

A 90 minute CX workshop should be developed by the CX Council to include information on the new CX initiative, service recovery, service standards, communication skills, etc.

Designated "best of the best" frontline personnel (cross-departments) are then chosen by their managers on a ratio of one advisor per 15–20 employees. CX Advisors then teach the CX workshop in teams of 3–4 to the entire organization. I believe that the message is far more powerful when presented by one's peers.

When the CX Advisors have had plenty of time to rehearse the workshop, schedule all employees in groups of no more than twenty employees (also depending on available room capacity) to attend this MANDATORY training over the course of a few months; there is no rush here.

Organizational Project Team

The leadership team should identify organizational-wide projects that will contribute to the success of a company-wide CX initiative. These projects might include service recovery standards, service behavior policies, sentence starters (so that all employees are 'telling the same story'), awards and recognition, or onboarding.

Make sure that every leader (manager, supervisor etc.) is placed on one, cross departmental team to carry out one of the projects. Place people on teams who don't normally work together. Make sure to establish milestones and a deadline for each team depending on the complexity of the project.

The CX Council oversees each project by way of the designated project coach. The goal of the project team is to develop the project to the point where it can be handed off to an appropriate person who will 'hardwire' it into your organization. For example, an onboarding project might be handed over to the VP of Human Resources for hardwiring and a service recovery project to the VP of Customer Service.

CX Initiative Launch

Make sure to have an official, company-wide CX initiative launch. Do this with much fanfare and ensure that everyone knows that the goal is to become the employer and the vendor of choice. I have witnessed themed parties, organization-wide picnics, and even a company parade to hype this initiative. Make it high-profile and a high priority.

Departmental CX Projects

After the CX Advisors have taught the workshop to all employees and after the organizational team projects are underway, begin to drive the CX initiative at a departmental level. Gather departmental heads and challenge them to meet with their teams to establish short-term projects to better the customer experience from their perspective. Encourage them to go after the 'low hanging fruit' first; those touch points that they have already recognized as ones which need to be tweaked. These departmental projects will be on-going so make sure not to overwhelm any manager/supervisor by trying to get these done too quickly.

Finally, make sure to celebrate small successes along the way. Recognize your CX Council members, your CX Advisors and your entire staff at appropriate times. Keep the momentum going and have fun with this.

Social media gives companies a channel that's great for proactively delighting customers. While most customers who connect via social media may assume a company is too busy to engage over social media, for the company, being able to learn about customer issues instantly on social media can be an opportunity to create a great customer experience.

In this story from LinkedIn, a man named Mike McCready tweeted a picture of his room view at Delta Hotels' Vancouver Suites. He included the caption, "The inside of my room at the Delta is really nice, but the view, not so much."

Mike wasn't expecting to hear anything, especially since he didn't include the Delta Twitter handle in his tweet. But within less than an hour, he received a tweet.

Delta wanted to put Mike in a new room. But since he was leaving the next day, Mike told them that switching rooms wouldn't make much sense.

The hotel staff wasn't satisfied with leaving it alone. When Mike returned to his room later that day, he found a handwritten note and pastries.

Mike would probably still have a positive opinion about Delta Hotels without their tweeting or pastries. But he wouldn't have raved about the company.

Thus, for the cost of a few pastries, Delta Hotels left a strong impression on a customer with a huge return shared on social media a high return.

CRITICAL QUESTION #11

What's Next In CX?

FORRESTER RESEARCH'S REPORT, *'Does Customer Experience Really Drive Business Success?'*, emphasizes that, when companies offer significantly differentiated customer experiences, consumers are more compelled to switch or stay, while those who provide poor CX demonstrate reasons to defect. Therefore, leaders are eager to improve upon their current CX offerings, and laggards are motivated to catch up to (and possibly surpass) their competition. But, how should these brands go about bringing their CX strategy to the next level in an effort to further loyalty and retention?

I recently had the opportunity to have a "fireside chat" at a conference held virtually, with CX experts around the world. I thought I would share the questions and my answers exactly as they were presented. The goal was to explore the present state of CX and how companies can sustain momentum as the space evolves.

Question (from audience): What is the state of customer experience strategy today? Is it a primary differentiator for a brand?

My reply: I'm not sure it's the primary differentiator. It's a critical component, but companies still must have a clear picture of their target customer and value proposition. Our data shows that customer expectations are rising faster than most companies' ability to improve their customer experience. This creates an experience desire gap, allowing companies to step in and grab more business if they can improve the customer experience. And as customers become more aware of the experiences that they want, they will expect all of the companies they work with to meet their needs. This puts all companies on notice, because they are being compared against industry leaders such as Amazon and USAA, not just against their industry peers.

Question: With the influence of social media, how is this affecting CX?

My reply: In this world of social media, companies must now 'earn the right' to business growth by delivering an experience that customers want to have again and tell others about. This means that the brand has to 'prove' its messaging and brand attributes on a consistent basis with customers, through their interactions with customers. The experience delivered to customers IS the brand, and that is what they message to the world on social media forums and with friends and colleagues.

The relationship status between customer experience and social media would likely be set to 'It's complicated.'

Although social media provides new, exciting ways for brands to connect with consumers, businesses have also found that customers can be quick to air their complaints on social sites. And, in the days before social customer care strategies were more commonplace, many brands found themselves drowning in damage control as negative posts about their products, services, and company spread virally across the web.

Over time, businesses began to view Twitter, Facebook, Instagram, and their ilk as valuable customer service channels, and developed action plans for engaging with customers via the online sites they frequented. While the benefits have been realized, one major challenge remains: how to keep pace with evolving social trends.

I can identify three major trends in the customer experience space.

1. Tapping into private communities

Private communities, like Slack and Discord, are quickly becoming important channels for customer care. These channels either require users to request permission to join, or they need to have the proper link to access the server—a far cry from the traditionally public forums of Twitter and Facebook.

Through velvet rope communities like these, brands can set up a customer forum where users can ask questions and find answers to their customer service queries.

2. YouTube: it's more than just cat videos

With 1.59 billion daily active users, Facebook remains the most popular social site—but a third of all internet users watch more than a billion hours of video every day on YouTube. Further, Trust Insights and Talkwalker measured interest in major social sites based on search volume and found that YouTube had the most account creation searches, followed by Discord, Instagram, Facebook, and Slack, in that order. These factors, among others, makes it an ideal channel for promoting your brand's videos, partnering with influencers to expand your exposure, and conducting social listening to get a read on your customers.

Also, by encouraging customers to visit your brand's YouTube channel for self-service content, you can reduce the strain on your contact center. For example, Citizens Bank uses its YouTube account to share "Overdraft 101" videos that tackle subjects like 'overdraft plan options' and those that answer basic customer inquiry questions like 'Why did I get that fee?' Similarly, Nintendo uses YouTube to post videos about issues like how to set up a family membership for its Nintendo Switch devices.

3. The growing link between social and search

Social and search are becoming closely linked, particularly YouTube and Google (which are owned by the same company). YouTube videos, and other user-generated content is increasingly being featured by search engines as well.

Social media management platform Hootsuite conducted an experiment to determine whether social media has a positive impact on search engine rankings. The company discovered a "strong correlation between social activity and rankings." Hootsuite adds that quality is more important than quantity when it comes to social media posts.

I know I have given you the long answer, but I have to add a caveat...you must monitor social media activity to ensure it's current and correct, because outdated or negative content can affect your brand reputation. In addition to the obvious channels, be sure to stay on top of public forums like Quora, which customers use to ask questions and to post reviews. With more than 300 million monthly users and content that often appears in search results, it behooves brands to include it as part of their content moderation strategy.

Social media is in a constant state of flux. While there's no guessing what new channels will emerge, the power of these three trends suggest they've earned a place in your customer service strategy.

Question: Do you feel that CX makes an organization more accountable to their customers?

My reply: Customer experience has led to increased access to information for customers, empowering them in selecting, buying, and using products and services. It's led, as well, to reductions over time of other forms of differentiation, such as lower cost sourcing and product innovation. It means company and brand reputations are being built in a more transparent environment where all parts of the organization can make or break that reputation, so the weakest link becomes the most important.

I get requests to complete surveys quite often. They come from my bank, after in branch transactions; websites I visited; customer service of my credit cards and cable providers. They all want to know how I would score whatever is important to *them*, and leave a little space for *my* comments. Some of these surveys are just two or three questions long, but others expect me to answer pages of seemingly repetitive and circular questions.

I have never seen a survey request that explains why my opinion is so important to them. In other words, they never indicate what is going to happen after I've completed the survey, carefully answered all the questions, and provided very detailed comments. Presumably, if the tabulated scores are high enough, whoever created or sponsored these surveys, will high five each other and cash their bonuses. But what about my needs? Would my contribution help anybody to make a better selection? How would I know if my responses contributed to a better product or service? Sometimes a company proudly advertises their customer satisfaction success, but I wonder if their claims can be taken seriously because there is no way for a consumer to validate them. For these reasons I stopped answering survey requests a long time ago.

Amazon is considered by many the poster child of customer centricity. I have done business with Amazon for over ten years and made hundreds of various purchases over that time. I cannot recall a single survey request from them, *ever*. Could it be, customer-centric Amazon does not care about the customer experience they provide? I think they don't survey their customers because they understand the power of authenticity that is growing fast with the advance of the social consumer. Amazon understood that consumers will never trust a brand more then they trust each other. A long time ago, instead of collecting self-serving survey ratings, they decided to enable their customers to share their experiences with each other in an open forum. Yes, over the years there were incidents of manipulation attempts. But, overall the customer reviews are extremely valuable to consumers who learned how use the reviews to reduce the uncertainty of their purchasing decisions.

According to the Keller Fay Group, two primary reasons customers write reviews and publish them online are:

1. Help other consumers to make the right choice for them—kind of: "*pay it forward*"

2. Help brands to improve their performance. Consumers rely on the transparency of their input to motivate brands to act.

I can only guess that since Amazon does not survey their customers, they probably use the content of reviews to measure the level of customer satisfaction of doing business with them.

So why do so many companies still shy away from exploring the content, provided by their customers without solicitation? The answers I've been given by CX executives over the years have a common thread:

*   Lack of control over the process

*   Doubts in authenticity of reviews

*   Fear of negative sentiments

In other words, it seems these companies do not trust consumers, who provide their feedback transparently. Yet, these very companies expect consumers to trust them with their feedback without any transparency at all. How reasonable is that?

Giving members of your team the leeway to do random acts of kindness for customers can make someone's day and create a buzzworthy customer experience.

Last year, as told by this story from Reddit, a Capital One customer discovered that Apple Magic Keyboards and orange juice do not mix. After the unfortunate spill, the keyboard was fine—mostly. The "2" key didn't work. And the numeral 2 was part of his account number with Capital One, which made logging into his online banking account impossible.

The customer figured he could just copy and paste a 2 from somewhere else, but Capital One, like many other financial institutions, restricts what you can copy and paste into secure fields.

Come to find out, a member of the Capital One support team saw the post on Reddit and decided to send "MaskedKoala" a brand new Magic Keyboard.

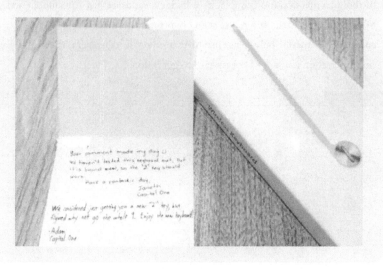

In a handwritten note, Janeth and Adam from Capital One explain how the bank thought about sending just the "2" key—but decided to go all out with a brand-new keyboard.

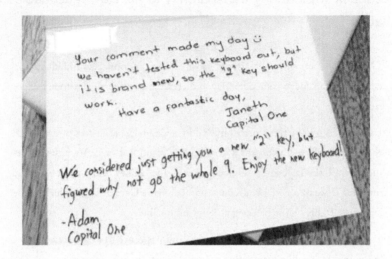

Your comment made my day ☺
We haven't tested this keyboard out, but
it is brand new, so the "2" key should
work.
        Have a fantastic day,
                    Janeth
                    Capital One

We considered just getting you a new "2" key, but
figured why not go the whole 9. Enjoy the new keyboard!

-Adam
Capital One

Showing customer love like this won't emerge from any formula of customer happiness. It's also difficult to mandate their execution in any way. These moments only happen if you give people the leeway to make them happen. Many of these companies, for example, have budgets set aside just for random acts of customer kindness. If a rep sees an opportunity to make things right for a customer, no matter how insignificant that one case may seem, they can use (up to a certain amount of) petty cash to get it done.

Question: What attributes define companies that lead the way with CX strategy? What qualities define laggards?

My reply: Companies that are differentiated start with customers' lives and what customers are trying to accomplish to guide how they will and will not grow. Customer emotions, needs, and objectives drive how leaders communicate, how they drive accountability, and how they unite their actions. These companies enable their employees to deliver value.

And, let me just focus on value for a moment. Every organization, no matter their size or scope, should be focusing on value if they are focusing on anything in CX. Imagine two boxes. One is huge. We'll call that COST. And, one is about one-fourth the size. We'll call that VALUE.

No matter what the initiative, the first question should ALWAYS be, "How do we increase the value versus the perceived cost of doing business with us?"

My assumption, although somewhat pessimistic, is that every one of our customers only have these two issues on their minds when they are deciding to do business with us. The cost is always greater than the value. Our number one job is to figure out how to increase that value box versus the size of the cost box.

I am not talking about price here. I am talking about how to creatively increase that value so that it throws up a blockade to entry by any competitor. I am talking about knowing that customer so well that we can customize our offering, therefore increasing the value.

Here's the problem. You have to KEEP increasing the value until you are sure that the value box is greater than the cost box. This may mean checking in with customers to get their feedback or just doing market research.

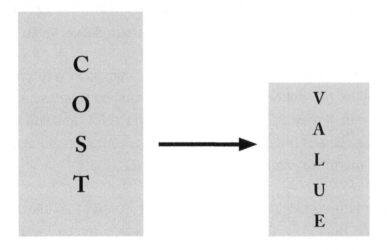

Sorry, I digress...Customer experience laggards continue to drive price differentiation as a strategy and cost containment in many instances. The silos lead the agendas often, and as a result, a separate and random experience is delivered to customers, which gets in the way of the customer feeling valued. The silos are working hard, but they are working hard separately. Without the perspective of a comprehensive understanding of customer needs and uniting efforts, companies stay on the same course to drive quarterly sales numbers, without necessarily developing a deep understanding of the customer experience that drives the ongoing growth or loss of the customer relationship and customer asset.

Research has identified four characteristics that separate customer experience leaders from laggards: **Purposeful Leadership, Compelling Brand Values, Employee Engagement**, and **Customer Connectedness**. Leaders operate more consistently with a clear and compelling set of values and vision for the future, their brand promises more explicitly guide how they treat customers, their employees are more committed to the success of the organization, and they more actively use insights about customers to drive decisions across their organizations.

Question: How can laggards catch up to leaders? Which CX improvements are critical to the success of such an overhaul?

My reply: Start by understanding the target personas of the customers. Study how they behave and what their requirements are. Keep seeking out what are the unmet problems these people encounter. Compare the results to how existing capabilities are delivered. The gap is the opportunity.

A good place to start is by honoring customers as the asset of the business. Unite leaders to care about the human lives—the customers coming in and exiting your business. Unite leaders in common definition and language in fearlessly discussing this one irrefutable outcome of the overall experience delivered by your company: Did your customer asset grow or shrink in the past month or quarter or year? Then, embed the empathy and caring with leaders to care about the "why?" Connect the dots between the reasons driving customers away and the actions and the ROI for leading customer experience improvement.

Customer experience is a reflection of an organization's culture and operating processes. So, any overhaul of customer experience needs to start internally. Customer experience laggards need to have a clear commitment to becoming more customer centric at senior levels, or any attempt at transformation will fall short.

Question: How can the element of surprise delight consumers and strengthen loyalty? Are consumers more likely to become advocates if they encounter CX when and where they least expect it?

My reply: Surprise is great, if it is delivered as an addition to a regular, reliable, and consistent experience that delivers on customer needs and provides peace of mind. In organizations where the experience is reliable (which are few), these moments of special experiences can breed memories that drive loyalty. But I am a huge advocate of first innovating on breeding moments of peace of mind. These will bring your customers the same type of joy and memories—and will earn word of mouth.

Delighting customers is overrated. It's hard to sustain because customers' expectations reset upward quickly and, in most cases, the customers biggest demand is that the core product or service quality lives up to promises. Therefore, <u>consistency of delivery and meeting requirements for all matters more</u>. Exceeding expectations is more important and may be about turning around a mistake more than about delighting. Customers become advocates over time when the organization is trustworthy and follows the golden rule consistently of treating others as you would wish to be treated. If expectations are exceeded, then that increases the odds they will become an advocate. The best chance of exceeding expectations is when a customer is under stress or there has been a service failure that can be rectified quickly.

So, what I am saying is that surprise and delight is great, but it will only have a lasting effect on customers if companies also consistently meet their basic needs. It doesn't do any good to try and surprise a customer if you're likely to let them down on the next interaction. The key is to understand what customers are really trying to accomplish and help them do that. Think about any touch point as part of a customer's broader journey. If you can help them get what they want, instead of just trying to surprise them, then you can build real loyalty.

Question: What strategic CX innovations can we expect to see in the near future? How will these changes impact how consumers engage with their favorite brands?

My reply: The importance in this stage of customer experience is for companies to not think of this work as a program, or 'one and done.' The innovation will be, quite frankly, for companies to stay the course this time around and embed customer experience as a competency in their business.

The innovations we see will be how organizations deliver on continuity of experience. The ability to succeed on this mass personalization at scale will differentiate the winners and the losers. There are hundreds of innovations per year in improvements in customer experiences worldwide. What's important for most organizations is to keep an eye on what others have done to innovate: a) in their industry and geography; b) in other geographies in the same industry; and c) then looking at other industries, as many ideas can be replicated without coming up with entirely unique innovations.

These changes, however, depend on the type of innovation. If the innovation improves personalization, modifies employee behavior, enables better feedback from customers, improves the ability for the organization to act as one, redefines processes from the outside in, improves openness, or designs the experience in a better way, then consumers and business customers will be able and want to engage more.

To answer your question directly, there are several trends that are creating the opportunity for more CX innovations. The rise of mobile devices will continue to allow companies to redesign their interactions with customers in new ways. Yes, lots of companies already have mobile sites and mobile apps, but that's not a real innovation. Companies will more radically rethink how they interact with customers and how they design their products and services. To get a sense of this, all you have to do is look at how Uber has changed the taxi experience.

To keep up with customers, you need to tackle today's pain points—but that's not enough. CX leaders also should envision the experience they want their customers to enjoy tomorrow—and use today to build it.

EPILOGUE

THE ATTENTION FOR customer experience has grown exponentially over recent years—and it keeps doing so with customer experience now being recognized as an essential focus to create business and customer value.

Yet, at the same time, customer experience has become a "thing," a term many people use for various reasons.

People are at the center of all business success. It sounds obvious, but in times of digital transformation, one can easily forget it. We're more than our demographic, behavioral, and other data—and while data have become increasingly important for customer experience optimization, it's important to look beyond the dashboards as well.

> *"The customer isn't king anymore; the customer is dictator"*
>
> — *Gerry McGovern*

The expectations of people have also changed. The ubiquity of digital platforms in their—our—lives is one of many factors impacting shifts in behavior and demands. We have even started speaking about a digital customer experience.

However, all in all, the essence of CX and customer experience management hasn't changed all too much because, in the end, customer experience—the experience part—is all about emotions. So, let's take a look at that essence. And why customer experience keeps becoming more important and so many organizations still struggle to meet those expectations.

The definition of customer experience hasn't changed a lot either. In a nutshell, it's still seen as both individual and holistic *(cumulative, over a longer period)* perceptions and feelings customers have when interacting with any component of your brand and service of your company: support, products, people *(employees)*, applications, marketing, systems, and more.

In a sense, everyone is a customer: customers as buyers, employees, suppliers, and other stakeholders.

Whether it's in their capacity as consumers, citizens, hotel guests, members, patients, or workers, people and the ways you serve and empower them are key to future business growth. All parts of your organization and ecosystem need to be connected and aligned with the optimization of customer experience(s) as the drivers of revenue and enablers of value for people you interact with.

The exploding attention for customer experience, as such, is great. It—theoretically—shows that organizations are starting to put their customers more at the center: customer-centricity.

Not in the original sense of focusing on your best customers but in the sense of optimizing your processes and business functions around the customer. And not just in an all too theoretical and strategic way but in practice, in real life, in service and beyond.

The end-to-end customer experience

The definition of a customer has changed. Or at least: we need to think differently about the customer. In a connected business reality, everyone in the ecosystem of your business is a customer: from employees and investors to partners, buyers, and their networks, including the various players in the value chain from manufacturer to end consumer and back. In other words: all stakeholders.

Customer experience is crucial for the present and future of your business. It always has been but in an era of a more autonomous and 'empowered' customer who has higher expectations, it is even more so.

In that famous connected—and increasingly digital—age we live in, the determining factors shaping the experiences we have with businesses are multiplying. We used to only look at face-to-face contacts, interactions across several channels, customer service, products and solutions, the brand as such and other attributes, all close to the business, as being crucial elements of the customer experience—as the sum of all experiences.

In reality, the end-to-end customer experience is defined by much more than that. In fact, the customer experience is shaped by numerous factors that escape the "control" of a business. Think about word-of-mouth, to name just one. At the same time customers, don't always want an experience in the 'wow' sense we often give it. Sometimes they just want to come in your shop, get their product, pay and get out asap. They want ease over delight.

The key reason why the customer experience will never be 'in control' is because customers are individuals and the core element in the customer experience equation is highly emotional, personal, contextual, and diverse.

Customer experience management: value is in the eyes of the beholder

So, the term "customer experience management" (CEM)—literally managing customer experiences—might seem somewhat of a weird term at first sight and maybe even out of touch with a changing reality.

Sure, you can manage many elements that create the conditions for fantastic customer experiences: the quality of your customer service, the response speed of your contact center representatives, the content you create, the quality of the various inbound and outbound interactions (not in a marketing context but a general context of inbound and outbound communications), the brand narrative, the touch points where different interactions occur, the overall "ambience" of physical experiences, deep insight into what customers want, the list goes on and will grow.

However, **you cannot really "manage" the customer experience as such. And the reason is simple: customers shape their own experiences.**

Individual customers are all different. As customer experience is really "owned" by the customer, vendors of CEM solutions, marketers, and many others have started talking about customer engagement whereby there is (inter)action instead of customer experience (both are not the same).

This complexity, along with the lack of understanding what customer-centricity really means and the fact that in reality it often remains a promise (let alone, siloed effort), has been creating the famous customer experience gap. Of course, customer experience management is about more than what I just mentioned here. I used the 'management' part of it to make a point—strictly speaking, customer experience management is about "design" for the kind of experiences you (no, wrong: your customers) value and want, from the most obvious low hanging fruit to the more sophisticated parts of the puzzle, and it's always emotional.

Even if customer experience is about emotions and individual parameters, there are many commonalities in the ways people experience things, fulfil a task, and value experiences.

Customer experience management and the outside-in view

Customer experience management or CEM is not about managing customer experiences as such, but a practice that includes the design of customer interactions—and touch points—aiming to meet customer expectations and ideally exceed them (when it makes sense), whereby the end-to-end customer experience is taken into account and the mutual value of customer interactions is optimized in a continuous loop of interaction, reaction, pro-action, and optimizing satisfaction to go beyond "good enough."

Given the many dimensions and elements in the overall customer experience, it does require management, transformation and process optimization, involving the customer on various levels, making intensive use of data and information, and removing obstacles and silo effects, taking into account—and involving—the customer, and increasingly deploying connected technologies. Mind you: it's not just about data and technology. It's still about good old but hard to achieve "putting yourself in the shoes of" and "having an outside-in view." Customers are more than data and digital feedback; they also walk around and can speak. And remember: they have emotions!

The customer experience gap: enabling better customer experiences

Our inability to approach customers as individuals and our traditional lack of understanding of what customers really want, along with an underestimation of the emotions of the customer, further strengthened the customer experience gap: the gap between how businesses think about the customer experiences they offer and the value of the customer experience in the eyes of the beholder, the customer.

The customer experience gap has always been and remains huge. You can look up hundreds of pieces of research from at least the last decennial and it will always come back.

The percentage of business respondents claiming they offer (or better: enable) "a good customer experience" is dramatically higher than the percentage of customers saying they experience these experiences as good (or great for that matter).

In "How to achieve true customer-led growth – Closing the delivery gap," an e-book published by Bain & Company, James Allen, Barney Hamilton, Rob Markey, and Frederick F. Reichheld found that **80% of companies believe they provide a superior proposition with only 8% of customers agreeing**.

Does this mean you can't have a strategy to improve customer experience? Does it mean you cannot manage customer experiences to a specific degree? Not at all. There is a whole lot you will ALWAYS be able to do in order to ENABLE great customer experiences.

You probably noticed the words ALWAYS and ENABLE are in capitals. Here is why:

- **The enablement of great/easy customer experiences is never finished**. It stretches much further than, for instance, marketers believe. Other reasons: customer expectations change, customer expectations differ, there will always be bad decisions, and none of your employees will ever be perfect. Finally, with each new technology, channel, societal evolution, etc., both customer expectations and the factors defining customer experience will continue to change as well.

- **You can and should create the conditions for WOW customer experience and of course customer service**. But you can't fully control the perceived value to the customer. You can optimize everything you do—and should do it as well, in a prioritized and realistic way—but you will never be able to satisfy everyone. This is where listening to your customer and continuous loops of gathering feedback and data to enhance what you do comes into play, again adding to the 'always' aspect.

So, what can you do? How can you put the customer experience in the center of what you do and should you even care?

A more holistic and connected customer experience approach going beyond marketing and customer service is essential to succeed. But that isn't enough.

Personalized service makes customers feel special. When you include a customer's name in an email or send them a hand-written birthday card, they feel recognized and appreciated. Those positive feelings become associated with your company and voilà—you have a happy, loyal customer.

Spotify user Jelena Woehr received that individualized touch sending the music service some positive feedback in an email. To thank her, a member of the Spotify team created a custom playlist for her. Take a look:

Notice anything about the titles? They spell out a message: **"Jelena/You Are Awesome/Thanks a Lot/For These Words/It Helps Me/Impress/The Management."** Clever!

Woehr was wowed and posted the playlist to Facebook. "Oh my god," she wrote, "Spotify customer care is ADORABLE." As Woehr's reaction shows, gestures mean more to customers when they are personal.

Why and how customer experience matters (more)

Let's recap why customer experience matters. We all know the obvious answers as I have repeated time and again:

- Customer expectations have increased

- People have more channels to voice their opinions

- Failing to deliver upon customer expectations makes people change vendors, especially in specific industries

- Study after study shows that CX will increase profits

In fact, across every industry I've been working with lately, customer experience is at the top of the corporate agenda.

Customer experience is contextual

Not all individual experiences have the same impact on everyone: people are different.

This doesn't mean that a few bad experiences by definition are disastrous. There are even numerous examples where customers don't change vendors, even if they have bad customer experience upon bad customer experience.

This has to do with many factors, ranging from an exclusivity of a company within its niche, the difficulty of switching vendors and the 'positivity' of the overall customer experience, to very human factors such as the need for comfort (and thus no change) or even the affinity with a brand.

Furthermore, there are differences—regional, regarding industry, etc.—that make the impact of the customer experience less or more important. It might seem counterintuitive but it's a fact: some companies suffer far more from poor customer experiences than others.

The customer dictates the what and how

However, in general the importance of the customer experience has grown, as has its impact on the bottom-line of organizations. And the increasing expectation of customers—in general—is far from a fad. Everything needs to be better and faster for Generation Now.

The customer does increasingly dictate what he wants, spoiled by customer experiences offered by best-performing organizations or across industries that have focused on the customer experience early on.

Customer experience, ownership and leadership

The good news is that no one 'owns' the customer experience, in any given industry, except the customer. Yet, customer experience excellence requires leadership, executive prioritization, and an enterprise-wide approach, with a clear place for customer experience in your culture.

I hope that I have shared these in the book but here are several reasons for the need to have executive leadership and bring the customer and customer experience into the boardroom.

- Customer experience is key in virtually all customer-facing processes and activities: from customer service and customer retention to loyalty and engagement.

- Research by several companies clearly indicates what most suspect: there is a clear link between customer experience success and CEO leadership involvement.

- Customer experience is the essence of the future growth of the organization as more research clearly indicates. There is a clear link between business performance and C-level customer experience involvement.

- Customer experience and employee engagement go hand in hand. Employee engagement requires leadership, as studies have confirmed.

- The change and strategy required to focus on the customer and customer experience can't happen without C-level direction.

Everyone plays a part in achieving customer experience excellence but some do more than others. A variety of roles has been on the rise over the past few years to make customer focus a reality and customer experience enhancement more than lip service. These responsibilities are shared but there always needs to be leadership.

We live in a world of gaps and it should be your mission to close these gaps by building bridges in your organization, with your customers and across the entire ecosystem of your business.

- There are gaps between what we believe customers want and what they actually want.

- Gaps between how we perceive the quality of the customer experiences we enable and how customers perceive the value of them.

- Gaps between the front end of our businesses and the back office.

- Gaps between divisions.

- Gaps between brand promises and brand experiences.

- Gaps between the ways we seek business value and the ways we offer and benefit from customer value.

Even if our organizations become more customer-centric and we connect processes, people, information and things, we are far from where we should be. It proves to be hard to be more agile and adapt to an increasingly real-time economy. It proves to be hard to catch up with the realities of technology and demanding customers, including our employees. And it certainly is hard to prioritize how we can create more business value by offering more customer value.

One of the many reasons contributing to these gaps, to this Swiss cheese full of holes, is the disconnect between several business functions. Another reason is the disconnect between processes and divisions that try to achieve comparable goals, without trusting each other, let alone collaborate. Yet another reason is the fact we often sell the importance of customer experience the wrong way and don't get the buy-in. A final one is our never-ending urge to control, fear of losing control, and overprotection of the silos we create.

It's about integration and relationships between people through connected processes and working across silos, having a much broader perspective, involving the whole business, customers, and ecosystem. Because **the customer experience is the task of EVERYONE and, in the end, RELATIONSHIPS make the difference**. Technology simply enables us to do it better.

Optimizing the customer experience: the holistic and integrated must

Customer experience optimization is a holistic task, involving the whole organization and looking at the customer as an individual, not as an email address or a series of—often disjointed—contact moments.

The most direct interactions with and experiences of customers occur in the front end and across customer-facing operations. Think about the help desk (customer service, contact center), sales, face-to-face interactions, and even some marketing communications.

Part of the customer experience optimization exercise is to connect the front office and the back office. In practice this is often not the case.

Two examples:

1. If a contact center agent doesn't dispose of the right information to service a customer because crucial data are missing to get a full customer (interaction) view, the disconnect between the back office (where information enters) and the front end (where information enters too but where at the same time direct customer contact occurs) leads to frustration and poor experiences.

2. When a customer engages directly with your business by using an online tool, the underlying process-

es in which the tool plays a role should be aligned, fast, and supportive of the intent the customer had when using it. If this isn't the case, the initial positive experience when using the tool loses all meaning if the processes and systems it is used for are slow.

While the disconnect between the front office and the back office is among the main cause of customer dissatisfaction, there are many—often relatively easy—ways to improve the customer experience. Yet, it takes a deep understanding of what customers truly want instead of assumptions and that also means customer experience metrics and measurement.

Customer experience transformation: getting started

So, improving the customer experience ranks high on the agenda of many organizations and executives. Because it's important, because competition is getting better at offering great customer experience, and because 'okay' isn't good enough anymore for numerous reasons, the customer being the main one.

As customer needs evolve, and as their understanding of the competitive landscape expands, you need to rethink many of the systems and processes that have been set over the years, driven primarily by the needs of the company rather than by the desires of your customer. With increased competition from an array of sources in virtually every industry, and significantly increased customer expectations for service, it's time for you to take a step back and reorganize around the needs of your customers.

The key word here is "reorganize." That's because the delivery of customer experience cuts across the many silos that exist within any company of size. In brief, this is not an issue just for the marketing department or for human resources. The process of creating and delivering a consistent, differentiated, and branded customer experience will affect almost every aspect of a company's operations.

An example of real-world customer experience

Let's look at the handoff between sales and operations as one final example. In recent work with a major manufacturer, the one-on-one relationships developed during the sales process were found to be a key component of the decision to enter a business relationship. For sales, you get there by building trust, establishing a strong relationship, and identifying—then dismantling—barriers.

Following a letter of agreement and "post deal" dinner and congratulations, the prospective client was handed off to the next stage of the onboarding process; the formality of finalizing a contract. For legal, the process is (and clearly I'm oversimplifying here) about "winning." While the deals were closed for the most part, the process was a negative experience for the new customer, in no small part because it was unexpected and inconsistent with their prior experience. Why? The goals for sales and legal aren't in alignment.

IT wasn't operating from the same playbook as either legal or sales, though that's a slightly longer story. What's important to understand is that the lack of a defined customer experience strategy across these critical functions created perceptual issues that in some cases never went away. The long-term results were lower levels of initial satisfaction, and the creation of an "us vs. them" perception that colored the relationship for some time.

I am not naïve. Organizational goals for customer experience in the pre-purchase and post-purchase phases of a customer relationship are different. Understanding all customer-facing functions is critical for driving a customer experience that also delivers desired business results. In some companies, I've encountered the perception that experience = cost. In fact, I've seen the opposite. Good customer experience = profit.

Moving away from the process-driven approach of interacting with customers based on a structured, "this is how we do it" model, to a more flexible, customer-focused perspective based on the question, "how should we do it?" aligns customer needs with business realities.

This isn't a process that can typically be done quickly or easily. Nor is it a process that can be handled by a single group. The cross-functional nature of delivering experience dictates a cross-functional approach to defining and implementing it. In short, **customer experience isn't a function or a department—it should become the center of everything you do.**

WORKBOOK

Ok, now it's time to put into practice the principles you have learned in this book. The following pages are designed for you to ask your team/organization the ten critical questions and for you to start to gather feedback from frontline, middle management and the leadership team.

CRITICAL QUESTION #1

Why should you start thinking about shifting from customer SERVICE to customer EXPERIENCE?

_____

_____

_____

_____

_____

_____

_____

_____

_____

_____

_____

_____

_____

_____

CRITICAL QUESTION #2

What's The Difference Between Service and Experience?

_____

_____

_____

_____

_____

_____

_____

_____

_____

_____

_____

_____

_____

_____

_____

CRITICAL QUESTION #3

Why Customer Experience?

_____

_____

_____

_____

_____

_____

_____

_____

_____

_____

_____

_____

_____

_____

_____

_____

_____

_____

CRITICAL QUESTION #4

How Do We Change our Perspective?

_____

_____

_____

_____

_____

_____

_____

_____

_____

_____

_____

_____

_____

_____

_____

_____

_____

_____

CRITICAL QUESTION #5

How Do I Get My People More Engaged?

_____

_____

_____

_____

_____

_____

_____

_____

_____

_____

_____

_____

_____

_____

_____

_____

_____

_____

CRITICAL QUESTION #6

How Can We Understand Our Customer Better?

_____

_____

_____

_____

_____

_____

_____

_____

_____

_____

_____

_____

_____

_____

_____

_____

_____

CRITICAL QUESTION #7

What Can Our Customers Tell Us?

_____

_____

_____

_____

_____

_____

_____

_____

_____

_____

_____

_____

_____

_____

_____

_____

_____

_____

CRITICAL QUESTION #8

How Do We Measure Customer Experience?

_____

_____

_____

_____

_____

_____

_____

_____

_____

_____

_____

_____

_____

_____

_____

_____

_____

CRITICAL QUESTION #9

How Do We Respond to Negative Feedback?

_____

_____

_____

_____

_____

_____

_____

_____

_____

_____

_____

_____

_____

_____

_____

_____

CRITICAL QUESTION #10

Where Do We Get Started?

_____

_____

_____

_____

_____

_____

_____

_____

_____

_____

_____

_____

_____

_____

_____

_____

CRITICAL QUESTION #11

What's Next in CX?

_____

_____

_____

_____

_____

_____

_____

_____

_____

_____

_____

_____

_____

_____

_____

_____

_____

ABOUT THE AUTHOR

CERTIFIED SPEAKING PROFESSIONAL, Jeff Tobe's credentials are impressive. Insider Magazine dubbed him "The Guru of Customer Experience" and readers of Convention & Meetings Magazine chose him as one of their favorite speakers along with other celebrities including Bill Clinton, Anderson Cooper, Condoleezza Rice and Daniel Pink. He is a customer experience and employee engagement expert, professional speaker and bestselling author who works with companies and organizations who want to increase their bottom line by changing their customer experience and retaining great talent.

Tobe founded Coloring Outside the Lines in 1994 and since then has worked with hundreds of clients ranging from ones with less than 20 employees to Fortune 500 companies including Microsoft, PepsiCo, Bank of America, ReMax International and many more!

Jeff Tobe's most requested VIRTUAL or LIVE programs focus on CREATIVITY/INNOVATION, CUSTOMER EXPERIENCE and EMPLOYEE ENGAGEMENT. His high-energy, high-fun and high-content programs create the ideal presentation for any kind of corporate or educational forum.

More recently, Jeff started CES (Customer Experience Systems) through which they take medium-sized businesses through a one-year CX journey to make them the EMPLOYER of choice and the VENDOR of choice in their industry.

Jeff's articles have been read in hundreds of publications and he is the author of the hugely popular book, Coloring Outside The Lines. He is the co-author of three other books and his newest book, ANTICIPATE: Knowing What Customers Need Before They Do is quickly becoming one of the hottest business books on the market. He is also the creator of the Touch Point Focus initiative in which he helps organizations re-examine their customer touch points and change their customer experience.

Made in the USA
Middletown, DE
17 April 2022

64307168R00113